Melinda & Robert
Schoutens

FRESH AIR
ADVENTURES
SWITZERLAND

Fresh Air Adventures Switzerland
32 Unforgettable Activities

Melinda & Robert Schoutens

Texts and photography: Melinda & Robert Schoutens
Cover and layout: Jagna Pilczuk
Editor: Angela Wade
Proofreader: Karin Waldhauser

ISBN: 978-3-03964-051-5

First Edition: April 2024

© 2024 HELVETIQ (Helvetiq SA)
Mittlere Strasse 4
CH-4056 Basel

All rights reserved.

helvetiq.com

Melinda & Robert Schoutens

FRESH AIR ADVENTURES SWITZERLAND

32 Unforgettable Activities

To our children,

Life is a beautiful adventure with you both. As you continue on this journey, may you always take the time to appreciate and understand that:

- loving deeply is essential to a life worth living;

- life's greatest gifts reveal themselves in the simplest of pleasures;

- it's important to be kind to everyone and everything. Remember, we are all a little bit broken;

- you should stop to relish the moments that fill you with awe. Seek such moments often;

- good health is essential for a quality life. Create daily habits that foster robust health;

- you should fight for what you believe in, despite what others may think.

Thank you for choosing us,
Mom and Dad

> **It seems to me that the natural world is the greatest source of excitement; the greatest source of visual beauty; the greatest source of intellectual interest. It is the greatest source of so much in life that makes life worth living.**
>
> **SIR DAVID ATTENBOROUGH**
> BIOLOGIST, NATURAL HISTORIAN, AND AUTHOR

As always, we try to make a difference with the words we write and the excursions we highlight. We maintain our dedication of supporting the organizations that work tirelessly to help protect and preserve our only planet. We thank you for joining the adventures. Together, may we strive to protect our one and only home.

Contents

Map of Activities	9

CHAPTER I
The Need for Adventure — 11

CHAPTER II
Get Ready for Adventure — 15

What is adventure anyway?	16
How to safely prepare for adventure	17
Understanding trail markers	18
What to pack	19
Types of adventure	20
Risk profile	21
Helpful resources	22

CHAPTER III
Let the Adventures and Experiences Begin — 25

CHAPTER IV
The Transformative Power of the Mini Adventure — 215

CHAPTER V
The Best of Our Adventures — 219

Epilogue	222

Map of Activities

BL	01	🟢	**Augst**	Augusta Raurica—A Glimpse into Roman Life	27
	02	🟢	**Belchenfluh**	A Morning Adventure	33
BS	03	🟢	**Basel**	A Full Sensory Dining Experience	39
	04	🟡	**Basel**	Rhine River Swim	45
BE	05	🟡	**Grimsel Pass**	Adventures by Van	51
	06	🔴	**Grindelwald**	Epic Swiss Hiking Tour	57
	07	🔴	**Grindelwald**	A Flight to Remember	63
	08	🟡	**Interlaken**	Whitewater Rafting	69
	09	🟢	**Lauterbrunnen**	The Valley of Waterfalls	75
	10	🟢	**Oberried**	Swiss Bike Park	81
FR	11	🟢	**Lake Gruyère**	Stand-up Paddleboarding	87
	12	🟢	**Lake Murten**	Lake Murten Bike Tour	93
GR	13	🟢	**Chur**	Mountain Scooters	99
	14	🟢	**Chur**	Cross Golf Brambrüesch	105
	15	🟢	**Churwalden**	The Longest Toboggan Ride	111
	16	🟡	**Pontresina**	Guided Ibex and Marmot Tour	117
	17	🔴	**St. Moritz**	Alpine Mountain Biking Tour	123
LU	18	🟢	**Pilatus**	Camping in the Trees	129
OW	19	🟢	**Engelberg**	Bringing the Cows Up and Down the Mountains	135
SO	20	🟡	**Balmberg**	Balmberg Rope Park	141
TI	21	🟢	**St. Gotthard**	A Hidden Past	147
UR	22	🔴	**Andermatt**	Via Ferrata Diavolo	153
VS	23	🟡	**Fiesch**	The Hike That has it All	159
	24	🔴	**Fiesch**	Aletsch Glacier Tour	165
	25	🟢	**Saint-Léonard**	Underground Lake	171
	26	🟡	**Zermatt**	Blacknose Sheep and Ziplines	177
ZH	27	🟢	**Baar**	Höllgrotten Caves	183

Various Cantons:

	28	🟢	Disc Golf	189
	29	🟢	European Outdoor Film Tour	195
	30	🟢	Geocaching	199
	31	🟡	Sleeping Under the Stars	203
	32	🟢	Tour de Suisse	209

CHAPTER 1

THE NEED FOR ADVENTURE

> "
> One way to open your eyes is to ask yourself, 'What if I had never seen this before? What if I knew I would never see it again?'
> "
>
> RACHEL CARSON
> AUTHOR, MARINE BIOLOGIST, AND CONSERVATIONIST

With this book we encourage you to explore the experiential side of Switzerland. The side that allows you to discover its mountains, rivers, glaciers, trees, and meadows, and witness events that make this country an incredible place to play. We guide you through each activity using nature as our primary backdrop; in our opinion, it's the ultimate place for an adventure.

Over the past five years we've covered a broad spectrum of outdoor activities in our books: from family hikes to remarkable Swiss huts to winter exploration. It felt apt now to profile activities that embody a true sense of adventure. Conjuring up the perfect adventure can be time consuming! We remove the guesswork by highlighting some pretty fabulous activities for people of varying ages and abilities.

While the word adventure evokes an entirely different meaning to each individual and is greatly overused, adventure, in our eyes, means this: to break free from routine, try new things and, at times, safely push past your comfort zone. Some of the activities profiled fall under the category of cultural events that return us to the past or display deeply rooted traditions within Switzerland. They are all absolutely worthy of your time.

As we completed the research and participated in all of the activities highlighted in this book, something astonishing transpired: we felt a sense of wild abandonment and freedom. As adults, we moved away from the rigidity of our daily lives only to return to the enthusiasm that once encapsulated our youth. We wrote this book for individuals of all ages, knowing that the adults in the group might actually benefit more than the younger souls. If you find yourself flipping through the pages and eager to get out there, you are not alone!

It's time to embark on your own adventure and get your heart racing! Mae West, the famous actress and singer, once said, "You only live once, but if you do it right, once is enough!" We think she was right!

Melinda & Robert

CHAPTER II

GET READY FOR ADVENTURE

> "
> The whole purpose of an adventure is to gain some spiritual or emotional insight. When you compromise the process, you compromise the gain.
> "
>
> YVON CHOUINARD
> ENVIRONMENTALIST, OUTDOORSMAN, AND FOUNDER OF PATAGONIA INC.

Switzerland is a country rich with outdoor activities and cultural experiences. We've compiled a diverse selection of activities throughout the country with additional options; if you enjoyed a particular activity, we highlight more locations for further exploration.

When it comes to adventure, we recommend being receptive to new ideas, maintaining a free spirit and, in some cases, having a bit of courage!

What is adventure anyway?

Ask 10 people what the word adventure means to them, and we're certain you'll hear 10 unique definitions. For the sake of this book, we use the following points to guide us.

Adventures:

- leave us euphoric and longing for more;
- add excitement to our daily lives;
- help us feel alive and perhaps witness the familiar from a new perspective;
- often occur when nothing goes as planned: a missed train, flat tire, wrong turn, or unpredictable weather;
- happen when we least expect it;
- don't require us to be professionals, just willing to try new things.

Not all activities profiled fall into the category of adventure. We wanted to offer you an array of activities, so we also highlight a few cultural experiences. Some of the activities outlined require concentration, a certain level of fitness, courage, and an open mind; others provide alternatives in the way of spectator events. Those experiences offer a unique perspective and an emotional connection to this remarkable country.

We are keenly aware that we live in an era of extreme adventure, where, oftentimes, danger dictates the task. If you're an adrenaline junkie, a professional adventurer and/or thrive on insane quests such as, base jumping, climbing 4000 m peaks, or setting a speed record for scaling the Eiger, this is not the book for you! None of those activities are outlined here.

How to safely prepare for adventure?

There are inherent risks to outdoor exploration, it's as simple as that. We recommend that people participating in nature activities be healthy and physically fit. In addition, if you're a parent, you are always responsible for looking after your children, knowing their limitations, and ensuring their personal safety.

The best way to prepare for a day outside is to be responsive to new ideas. Discuss the adventure with your group to gauge everyone's comfort level. If your group is spontaneous and open to surprises, we encourage you to mix it up.

If you elect to adventure without a guide (only recommended for certain activities in this book), make sure you: have the right gear, understand all potential risks involved, check the latest weather conditions, and view available webcams. Confirm the area or route is open and safe for exploration. Never attempt to hike, bike, climb or explore an area that is closed; it is closed for a reason.

Please also pay careful attention in the mountains and the areas that surround them. They are extremely powerful. It is important to have some level of awareness of the location where your activity takes place, and the necessary skills required. As the Swiss landscape is changing drastically, it's always advised to check with a local or an expert beforehand and to be aware of the potential for rock falls, flooding, avalanches, and/or changing weather conditions.

When you hire a company or guide, do your research. Though we may recommend an organization because we had a positive experience with a particular guide, each experience will be different. We are not responsible for the companies, and their policies or guides, mentioned in this book.

Finally, for all outdoor adventures it's essential to know when to call it quits or to turn around. Placing yourself in harm's way is foolish and may cause injury. We assume no responsibility for individuals who read this book and participate in the activities and excursions: adventure at your own risk!

Understanding trail markers

Yellow: hiking trails

Hiking trails account for 63% of all trails in Switzerland.

Yellow trails are the easiest to navigate. They are generally wide and require the least amount of skill and equipment.

White-Red-White: mountain trails

Mountain trails account for 36% of all trails in Switzerland.

White-Red-White trails may be steep, narrow, have sharp drops, and/or edges. Handholds and/or chains provide stabilization on some trails.

White-Blue-White: Alpine trails

Only 1% of all trails in Switzerland are alpine trails.

White-Blue-White trails should be left to the experts. These trails require the most physical skill, equipment (rope, ice axe, compass, and crampons), and knowledge of Alpine terrain.

Trail maintenance, Trail closures, and changes to Trails

It's quite possible that some of the trails mentioned in this book are either under maintenance, closed due to weather conditions, or have changed over the course of time. To find out if the route you've selected is currently open and safe for exploration, check the "Useful resources" list (p. 22). Overnight accommodation options may also be under renovation or closed due to management changes or other reasons. Always contact any planned accommodation well in advance to ensure it's open and to secure your reservation.

Accurate information

We have done our best to provide accurate information in this book. We apologize if the information provided is no longer correct and would like to hear from you should this be the case (**info@helvetiq.ch**).

What to pack

On hikes, it's always advised to wear appropriate outdoor clothing and sturdy boots, and to pack layers of clothing to protect yourself should the weather change. Of course, your attire will be different for water activities, cycling, or those that require little physical exertion.

If the activity we highlight requires special equipment, it's included in the individual descriptions. It's always good to bring a backpack with the essentials; however, a backpack may not be required for every activity profiled.

Backpack checklist:

- Water for the duration of your journey
- Food and snacks
- Sun protection: sunglasses and sunscreen
- Hat (for warmth and/or to shield your face from the sun)
- Plastic bags (please take your trash with you if a trash can is not available)
- Wet wipes
- Knife
- Layers (fleece/raincoat/rain pants)
- Phone/camera/power bank
- Wallet
- Swiss Half Fare (Halbtax) and/or Junior cards if traveling with children
- Rega membership card
- First-aid kit
- Emergency phone numbers in Switzerland
  - **Ambulance: 144**
  - **Fire: 118**
  - **Police: 117**
  - **Poison: 145**
  - **Rega: 1414**

Types of adventure

Pictograms represent the type of adventure on offer. These icons include hiking, biking, camping, climbing, golfing, geocaching, underground, glaciers, whitewater rafting, stand-up paddleboarding, paragliding, waterfalls, destination/location, tobogganing, suspension bridges, overnight, and experience.

Cost

The general cost* of each adventure/excursion is highlighted in each write-up, using a pictogram.

 One coin (Inexpensive): free to CHF 25 per person

 Two coins (Moderate): from CHF 26 to 75 per person

 Three coins (Expensive): more than CHF 76 per person

Prices may be subject to change. Costs do not include public transport to and from each destination.

Age range

If traveling with children, the appropriate ages for all adventures are provided for each activity. In some cases, age has nothing to do with the required skill level to participate. You are responsible as a parent or guardian for gauging the skill level of your child.

Risk profile

As individuals, we all have varying levels of comfort that determine our interest in a particular activity. If you're traveling in a group or as a family, you may not all agree on what makes the ideal adventure, so we offer an array of activities to help strike a balance.

Green (Easy)

Start here to determine your individual risk profile. There's no need to rush, this is not a race. Green adventures often require little physical exertion, and may also have alternatives to choose from. We include cultural activities or festivals in this category. For example, Disc Golf or a spectator event such as *Alpabzug* (bringing the cows down the mountain) both require no gumption at all.

Yellow (Medium)

It's time to up your game! These adventures are ideal for those who enjoy some risk and are open to pushing themselves slightly out of their comfort zone. Yellow adventures may include whitewater rafting, stand-up paddleboarding, or suspension bridge crossings.

Red (Hard)

It's getting real! Get ready for a challenge that may induce sweaty palms and a racing heart. Red activities may include a ropes course, climbing, heights, speed, and other risk-assuming elements. Paragliding, glacier crossings, and via ferratas fall into this category!

Helpful resources

Tourist information

Local tourist information centers and websites should know about trail statuses for summer and winter activities, and provide additional information pertaining to the area.

Maps of Switzerland

Before you leave home, check this website to find out if your chosen trail is closed. Click on "Maps Displayed" and then "Closures Hiking Trails" (map.geo.admin.ch).

Swiss Hiking Trail Federation (Schweizer Wanderwege)

This website provides a plethora of helpful and practical information in German, French and Italian and detailed information on signalization for all seasons, hikes, snowshoe routes, and more (schweizer-wanderwege.ch).

SwitzerlandMobility app

This app provides detailed maps of Switzerland with over 65,000 km/40,000 mi of hiking routes within the country. Winter and summer activities, public transport stops, points of interest, a compass, and GPS are also included (schweizmobil.ch).

Swisstopo app

This free app offers detailed maps of all locations in Switzerland and gives users the opportunity to record routes for hiking, cycling, snow sports, and more. One of the app's best features is the ability to create your own route by selecting points that the app connects along the trail system (swisstopo.ch).

swissrent app

Consider downloading this app, which allows for easy rental of outdoor sports equipment, such as safety gear and clothing for biking, hiking, skiing and climbing (swissrentapp.com).

SBB Mobile app

Purchase tickets, check timetables, see schedule changes, and more on the user-friendly SBB Mobile app (sbb.ch).

 ### Rega app

Rega is the Swiss Air-Rescue service, providing emergency services and assistance in the mountains. The app is free and can be used within Switzerland and just beyond its borders. If you haven't signed up for Rega, we highly recommend you support this phenomenal organization. It's worth noting that it's funded exclusively by its patrons, and the yearly fee is reasonably priced (rega.ch).

 ### MeteoSwiss app

Provides information about weather in Switzerland, including a 24-hour forecast (meteoschweiz.admin.ch).

 ### Alertswiss app

This app immediately notifies you if there is an accident or danger in Switzerland. Free and helpful, it's good to have in the event of an emergency within Switzerland (alert.swiss).

 ### EchoSOS app

This is an emergency app that functions worldwide and is designed to provide the user with emergency calls, local emergency numbers and information pertaining to hospitals/emergency rooms in the local area (echosos.com).

CHAPTER III

LET THE ADVENTURES & EXPERIENCES BEGIN

> "
> The hardest mountain to climb is the one within.
> "

JIMMY CHIN
AUTHOR, FILMMAKER, PHOTOGRAPHER, SKIER,
AND PROFESSIONAL CLIMBER

Augusta Raurica – A Glimpse into Roman Life

CANTON:
Basel-Landschaft

LOCATION:
August

START AND END POINT:
Langgass

2+ HOURS

EASY

▶ ▶ ▶ Best time of year:

AUGUST

AGE RANGE:

4+

EQUIPMENT:

Sturdy shoes, sun protection

Overview:

The Romans occupied territories in Switzerland for close to six centuries. Remnants of that period in Swiss history can still be found today. The modern town of Augst, located in Basel-Landschaft, is built on the ruins of Augusta Raurica, the oldest known Roman settlement on the Rhine River. The area is a major tourist attraction and a place of research and study.

Take the bus to Augst BL, Langgass and walk up Giebenacherstrasse to Augusta Raurica. Trains stop at Kaiseraugst or Pratteln Salina Raurica, then the walk is about 1–1.5 km. It's best to arrive by public transport as parking is limited.

Augusta Raurica has a gorgeous amphitheater, the Roman House, a museum, an animal park, plus a lovely theme trail. As if that didn't warrant a visit, in late August, Augusta Raurica hosts Römerfest, a festival running for more than 25 years that transports you back in time. History enthusiasts will take particular delight in the gladiator fights, chariot races, markets and other "live" activities for people of all ages. The costumes worn are impressive pieces of art and this festival brings Roman history to life!

During Römerfest: Admission fees are charged and the price includes a round-trip with TNW (*Tarifverbund Nordwestschweiz*). Food is available for purchase and free shuttle buses run from Kaiseraugst train station. Find out more on the Augusta Raurica website.

Tips:

- The outdoor area of Augusta Raurica is open 365 days a year and worth visiting at any time, but Römerfest is particularly special.
- Have cash on hand, as there are no cash machines in the area.
- The small theme trail onsite is stroller-friendly and ideal for families.
- There is little shade. Be prepared for warm temperatures by bringing hats, sunscreen, and plenty of water.
- The museum (entry fee) and animal park are open daily from 10:00–17:00, except December 24, 25, 31 and January 1.
- It's possible to barbecue at designated locations.
- While in the area, visit the ruins beneath the St. Gallus church in Augst; access is a discreet entry on the Rhine River.

Contact Details:

Augusta Raurica
Giebenacherstrasse 17
4302 Augst
+41 61 552 22 22
mail@augusta-raurica.ch
augustaraurica.ch

More options:

+ **Museum Vindonissa, Brugg, AG**
  (vindonissamuseum.ch)
+ **Saint Pierre Cathedral, Geneva, GE**
  (site-archeologique.ch)
+ **Martigny, VS**
  (martigny.com)
+ **Abbey of St-Maurice, Saint-Maurice, VS**
  (abbaye-stmaurice.ch)
+ **Aventicum, Avenches, VD**
  (avenches.ch)
+ **Roman Museum, Nyon, VD**
  (mrn.ch)
+ **Musée Romain, Lausanne, VD**
  (lausanne.ch)

A Morning Adventure

🛡 **CANTON:**
Basel-Landschaft

📍 **LOCATION:**
Belchenfluh

START AND END POINT:
Langenbruck

2 HOURS

EASY

▶ ▶ ▶ Best time of year:

ALL YEAR

AGE RANGE:

ALL AGES

EQUIPMENT:

Sturdy shoes

Overview:

Watching the sunrise is always an extraordinary experience. Regardless of age, you can't help but be mesmerized by the stunning colors; it feels like the world slows down just long enough for you to savor the simplest and most profound aspects of life. For this sunrise adventure, wake up early, dress appropriately for the season, and pack some warm drinks and breakfast treats.

Belchenfluh is nestled between Eptingen, Waldenburg and Langenbruck, and straddles the cantonal borders of Basel-Landschaft and Solothurn. The area offers commanding views and, as the sun begins to peek over the horizon, you see the Alps in the distance.

You have to drive to this location as there's no public transport nearby. There are two parking areas with access to the trailhead. When walking the short distance from the parking lot, you have to walk on the road. From the trailhead on the road Schöntalstrasse/Bölchenstrasse (Google lists the road as Belchenpass), follow signs toward Belchenfluh. The trail continues uphill for about 1 km, then there's a series of stairs for the last 200 m. Once at the top, find the perfect spot to watch the magic unfold! Return using the same trail.

To make this more of an adventure, consider welcoming every new year with a sunrise hike! Or collect sunrise moments throughout the year!

Tips:

- + Access to this viewpoint is easy, making Belchenfluh the perfect sunrise location, but watch out for steep drop-offs at the summit.
- + Bring headlamps and/or flashlights to navigate in the dark. Wearing reflective gear is also a good idea.
- + Sunrises are best witnessed on clear days.
- + Please note that Belchenfluh and Belchenflue are synonymous. We saw both spellings for this area.

Contact Details:

Baselland Tourismus
Haus der Wirtschaft
Hardstrasse 1
4133 Pratteln
+41 61 927 6544
info@baselland-tourismus.ch
baselland-tourismus.ch

A MORNING ADVENTURE

More options:

+ **Overnight at Berggasthaus Schäfler, Schwende, AI**
+ **Brienzer Rothorn, Brienz, BE:** On Sundays in summer, the Brienzer Rothornbahn departs early.
+ **Overnight at Berghotel Faulhorn, Grindelwald, BE** (see p. 57)
+ **Overnight on Mt. Pilatus or Rigi Kulm, LU**
+ **Fronalpstock, Stoos, SZ:** This view over the lakes is not to be missed and is a personal favorite.
+ **Eggishorn, VS:** Early departures every Friday in summer. Stay for breakfast afterward!
+ **Riffelsee, VS:** Catch the Gornergrat Bahn from Zermatt to see the Matterhorn at first light.

A Sensory Dining Experience

CANTON:
Basel-Stadt

LOCATION:
Basel

START AND END POINT:
Tellplatz

2+ HOURS

EASY

▶ ▶ ▶ Best time of year:
ALL YEAR

AGE RANGE:
10+

EQUIPMENT:
Select your attire wisely!

A SENSORY DINING EXPERIENCE

Overview:

If you're looking for a special and powerful dining affair, look no further. The Blindekuh restaurants (there's another one in Zurich) are a sensory experience. More than just restaurants, Blindekuh is a foundation that works to connect sighted people with visually impaired people and offer meaningful work opportunities.

From the Tellplatz tram stop, walk down Bruderholzstrasse to the intersection with Dornacherstrasse. The entrance is 50 m up Dornacherstrasse. From the moment you're inside the restaurant, the experience begins. You place your belongings, including watches, jackets and bags, into a locker, then wait at a black curtain to be seated by the staff. Hold on to the shoulders of your waitperson, who guides you with ease to your seat: they are masters at navigating and making you feel comfortable. The dining room is completely void of any light. The waitperson explains where your utensils, glassware and plates are on the table. A staff member promptly takes your order and the night officially begins.

While dining, you start to notice how your other senses are heightened. Your sense of smell is activated, your hearing is amplified and your ability to orient yourself may be hindered. The dining experience is one of learning to let go, of trusting and empathizing with the seeing impaired. As you dine, you might just find yourself leaning into the person next to you or feeling the need to touch others, which is perfectly natural. As your other senses engage, discover how you personally respond to losing your sight, if only on a temporary basis: you might notice that your wine tastes richer and you can identify various flavors in your meal. The experience is powerful, to say the least, and brings a new appreciation for those with limited or no vision.

Blindekuh is not only a restaurant, but also has a bar and function room for special events for groups.

Tips:

- Arrive with an open mind.
- This is a powerful, multi-sensory experience for people of all ages. For some, it might be overwhelming. We took a while to relax, but once we regulated our breathing and felt safe, we fully embraced the experience for what it was.
- If you plan to take children, please communicate expectations of the evening in advance.
- This may not be the best experience for those who have trust issues or fear the dark.
- Check the website for opening hours and days.

Contact Details:

Blindekuh
Dornacherstrasse 192
4053 Basel
+41 61 336 33 00
blindekuh.ch

A SENSORY DINING EXPERIENCE

More options:

+ Dans le Noir?, Geneva, GE (geneve.danslenoir.com)
+ Blindekuh, Zurich, ZH

Rhine River Swim

CANTON: Basel-Stadt
LOCATION: Basel

START POINT: Tinguely Museum
END POINT: Kaserne

1 HOUR

MEDIUM

▶ ▶ ▶ Best time of year:

JUNE–SEPTEMBER

AGE RANGE: Must know how to swim

EQUIPMENT: Swimsuit, drybag, water shoes

 ## Overview:

Whether you live in Basel or visit during summer, swimming in the Rhine is an experience not to be missed. This mighty river runs from the Alps to the Netherlands for roughly 1300 km and becomes a hive of activity in the warmer months. You regularly see people swimming, relaxing, barbecuing or chilling on or in the water.

For an absolutely refreshing summer swim, fill a drybag with necessities and head to the entry point at Tinguely Beach. From the Tinguely Museum bus stop, cross the street to the museum, walk around the side and cross the bike path. The swimming starting point is just below you.

From there, float with the current for 3 km and see the city from a fresh perspective. If you prefer to swim with a guide you can go with a trained lifeguard. If you go without a guide, stay within the buoys and designated swimming zones for your safety. Keep a safe distance from all river traffic. Always look down stream; be aware of the ferries and never attempt to outswim them. It is essential to exit the water in the designated zones.

The exit point can vary, but you must exit, at the latest, at the fourth ferry and before the fourth bridge (Dreirosenbrücke) for safety reasons. It may be easier to exit at the Kaserne area at the third ferry, after the lower bridge (Mittlere Rheinbrücke).

Once out, have a shower and change into your clothes and head to one of the many buvettes (outdoor restaurants) along the river. Enjoy a drink or meal as you absorb the relaxed riverside vibe or stroll along the Rhine with a gelato in hand. It doesn't get much better than this!

 ## Tips:

- It's highly recommended that you are comfortable in open bodies of water and a strong swimmer. The Rhine maintains a swift current. Never swim alone.
- Lifeguards are available from 17:45 every Tuesday in July and August at Tinguely Beach. Advance bookings are essential (jfs.bs.ch).
- Wearing water shoes is highly recommended to protect your feet.
- Drybags can be purchased or rented from June to September for CHF 10 per day from the Tourist Office at Steinenberg 14, 4051 Basel. They are available in multiple sizes. Please be aware that the bag is not a lifesaving device.
- Pack two extra plastic bags in your drybag: one for your cellphone and the other for your wet swimsuit and towel.
- An official Rhine swim takes place every year, usually mid-August.
- There are a few showers available along the river for your convenience.
- Rheinbad Basel is also a great place to relax and take a plunge. If you spend the duration of your day on the river and hunger sets in, visit the adjacent Le Rhin Bleu restaurant (St. Alban-Rheinweg 195, 4052 Basel) for a meal or a drink. If you plan to dine at the restaurant, make your reservation in advance.

 ## Contact Details:

rheinschwimmen.ch

RHINE RIVER SWIM

More options:

+ Reuss River, Rottenschwil, AG
+ Marzili, Bern, BE
+ La Jonction, Geneva, GE
+ Jeunes-Rives Park, Neuchâtel, NE
+ Rhybadi, Schaffhausen, SH
+ Verzasca River, Lavertezzo, TI

Adventures by Van

CANTON: Bern
LOCATION: Grimsel Pass

START AND END POINT: Innertkirchen

1+ NIGHT

MEDIUM

▶ ▶ ▶ Best time of year:
JUNE–SEPTEMBER

AGE RANGE: 18+

EQUIPMENT: Driver's license, awesome music

Overview:

Van life has become very popular over the past decade. Having access to the open road and incredible nature makes traveling by van perfect for those looking for a flexible camping adventure.

The Grimsel Pass is the ultimate location for camping excursions. Not only is this pristine Alpine pass a delight for travel, it's also in close proximity to the Furka, Gotthard, and Oberalp passes. On this highlighted route, you have the opportunity to explore the region and all it has to offer.

Starting in Innertkirchen, begin your journey along the Grimsel Pass. Make the Gelmerbahn Funicular (advance bookings necessary; open from June to October) your first stop. Allow the 106% gradient up the mountain to fill you with excitement. Once at the top, get ready for a roughly two-hour hike (just under 5 km) around the impressive Gelmer Lake, situated at 1850 m. Once you've made the circular hike (White-Red-White mountain trail), board the funicular (check the time of the last descent) for the hair-raising, out-of-your-seat return ride.

Back on solid ground, cross over the Handeckfallbrücke for the short and well-marked hike to Hotel and Nature Resort Handeck for a delicious meal. Once satiated, head back over the hanging bridge and make your way to the Rhone Glacier–one of the most studied glaciers in the area due to its accessibility. Take the time for a tour. For a nominal fee, you can enjoy an easy walk in the area. There are multiple information boards in German and English.

Consider a visit to Grimsel Hospiz. This hotel provides a striking view of the Spitallamm Dam, which was constructed in 2019 and is expected to be completed by 2025. For those interested, a tour of the KWO Powerplant (advance bookings recommended) is a fascinating underground experience. Be prepared for cold temperatures as you learn more about hydroelectric power. Tours are available from June to October in German, or English upon request. Allow roughly two hours.

As the sun begins to fade, drive to the Handeggli parking spot for the night. Your overnight accommodation is located up the hill behind the Gelmerbahn Funicular parking lot. Space is limited. Park your van and pay the CHF 20 per night fee via PARK4NIGHT or by using the designated cash box. The fee is less if you camp with a tent. There are directions and rules for those spending the night in the area. Toilets are available onsite.

Locations such as the Grimsel Pass are magical. Not only is the pass the ultimate in terms of Swiss road trips, but the area is rich with activities and the opportunity to immerse yourself in nature (grimselwelt.ch).

 ## Tips:

- Cheeky Campers is based in the Basel region with plans of expanding to Bern and Zurich. It offers funky van designs with a simple rental concept: unlimited mileage, transparent costs/fees and ease of pick up and return via digital process on your cell phone. Vans come in two sizes: medium and large, with full roadside assistance throughout Europe. Bring your own bedding and food for the ultimate adventure.
- Be certain the location you selected to camp for the night is permissible.
- Our cost calculations consider van rental, overnight stay and tickets for excursions.
- When driving, headlights must be on at all times.
- Alpine passes may be difficult to navigate. Keep that in mind when planning your route.
- Credit cards are accepted at all gas stations. Fill up before driving any Alpine passes.

 ## Contact Details:

 cheekycampers.ch

 grimselwelt.ch

ADVENTURES BY VAN

More options:

- **Nomady** (nomady.ch)
- **Touring Club Schweiz** (tcs.ch)
- **Park4Night** (park4night.com)
- **Parkn'Sleep** (parknsleep.eu)

Epic Swiss Hiking Tour

CANTON:
Bern

LOCATION:
Grindelwald

START POINT:
Grosse Scheidegg

END POINT:
Schynige Platte

3 DAYS

HARD

▶ ▶ ▶ Best time of year:

JUNE–SEPTEMBER

AGE RANGE:

10+

EQUIPMENT:

Sleeping bag liner, toiletries

Overview:

This hiking tour is one of the most scenic in all of Switzerland! Starting at Grosse Scheidegg and ending at Schynige Platte, this three-day trek is a feast for the eyes. Each day offers impressive scenery and unforgettable views.

DAY 1:   7.5 km   3 h   463 m   259 m

Grosse Scheidegg–Distelboden–First

Day one is a beautiful trek that weaves over mountains, through meadows and, for almost the entire duration, at or above 2000 m/6562 ft. After arriving by bus at Grosse Scheidegg, the trail starts across the road from the Berghotel Grosse Scheidegg and parking lot. Several trails cross here; head toward First. The trail splits just after 1 km. Take the upper trail (White-Red-White) toward First. At approximately the 3.5 km mark, take the trail into the valley toward Chrinnenboden, through a valley with a marmot colony. Accommodation is at Berggasthaus First (2167 m). Rest assured; the crowds dissipate once the gondola retreats down the mountain for the evening.

DAY 2:   5.9 km   4 h   568 m   66 m

First–Bachalpsee–Burgihütte–Gassenboden–Faulhorn

From Berggasthaus First, walk toward the chairlift station Oberjoch in the field behind First. Follow the signs to Faulhorn. In less than an hour, you should arrive at Bachalpsee. Before you begin the climb to Faulhorn, linger on the lakeshore (inquire about picnic supplies before departing or when booking Berggasthaus First). Continue to the back of the lake and up the hill. Your destination today, Berghotel Faulhorn (2681 m), is quite a famous little place. Construction started in 1830 and was completed in 1833 by Samuel Blatter. Not much has been altered since! Dormitories were built to accommodate more guests in

EPIC SWISS HIKING TOUR

1957 and the use of mules to bring supplies up and down the mountain was eventually replaced by helicopter in 1982. The area is striking, with 360° views to the Eiger, Mönch and Jungfrau, the Vosges mountains in the Alsace, the Black Forest in Germany, and some of Switzerland's most beautiful lakes. Pull up a seat on the terrace, kick off your boots and order a drink to celebrate your arrival.

DAY 3: 10.2 km 5.5 h 205 m 910 m

Faulhorn–Männdlenen–Lauchera Grätli–Schynige Platte

On the final morning, rise in time to witness the sunrise, then enjoy a breakfast of bread, jam and coffee. Eat plenty to prepare yourself for the robust hike ahead. From Faulhorn, proceed down the switchbacks, turning right at the bottom toward Schynige Platte. The first 3 km/1.86 mi of this next section may still have snow in mid- to late July; use caution. Should you tire, look to the stunning views for motivation. Hikes with immense views like this are meant to be savored. The trail descends to Berghaus Männdlenen (food and toilets available). Once you arrive at Schynige Platte, be prepared for bustling activity. This mountain offers a great deal for visitors: the Swiss Flower & Panorama Trail, the daily alphorn concert, and if traveling with children, Lily's Treasure Hunt. Then board the train for the truly special trip down to Wilderswil.

TOTAL:

23.6 km   1236 m   1235 m   2861 m

EPIC SWISS HIKING TOUR

 **Tips:**

- This is a physically demanding hiking route. Please only attempt it if you're accustomed to hiking and have plenty of stamina.
- Book your stays far in advance. Never rely on a room being available without a reservation!
- White-Red-White: The mountain trails may be steep and narrow in some areas and may include sharp drops or edges. There is a small section that includes a steep descent with chain holds on the third day near Berghaus Männdlenen.
- This tour offers little shade. Pack plenty of water. Never rely on water being available on the trail. Drinking water is not available at Faulhorn, however, you may purchase bottled water. It's pricey, so be prepared.
- Faulhorn is only open from the end of June (depending on snow levels) until mid- to late October.
- Berghotel Faulhorn offers six double rooms, one four-bed room, plus two 30-bed dormitories. You can rent a sleep sack for CHF 7 if you do not have your own. There is a 22:00 bedtime curfew.
- Meal times are strict at the mountain inns. Please report to the dining halls at the designated times.
- Most credit cards and/or cash are accepted.
- Communal showers and toilets are available at Berggasthaus First. No showers are available at Faulhorn; however, rooms are equipped with cold water in jugs for tidying and brushing teeth.
- Visit First Cliff Walk for its views and sense of adventure.
- The free, daily (11:00–14:00) Alphorn concerts at Schynige Platte run from early July until October.
- Schynige Platte is also home to the Botanical Alpine Garden.

 Contact Details:

Berggasthaus First
Postfach 138
3818 Grindelwald
+41 33 828 77 88
administration@berggasthausfirst.ch
berggasthausfirst.ch

Berghotel Faulhorn
3818 Grindelwald
+41 79 534 99 51
info@faulhorn.ch
faulhorn.ch

EPIC SWISS HIKING TOUR

More options:

- Berggasthaus Schäfler, Schwende, AI
- Hotel Waldrand-Pochtenalp, Kiental, BE
- Berghotel Obersteinberg, Lauterbrunnen, BE
- Berghotel Bischofalp, Elm, GL
- Berghotel Tgantieni, Lenzerheide, GR
- Berggasthaus Heimeli, Sapün, GR
- Berghaus Sulzfluh, St. Antönien, GR
- Restaurant & Hotel Sankt Martin, Vättis, GR
- Capanna Corno-Gries CAS, Bedretto, TI

If you long for more hike-to-hut experiences, we've got you covered. In our book, *Fresh Air Kids Switzerland – Hikes to Huts*, we profile 36 mountain inns, hotels and Swiss Alpine Club (SAC/CAS) huts in impressive locations. We even include multi-day tours like this!

A Flight to Remember

CANTON: Bern
LOCATION: Grindelwald

START POINT: First
END POINT: Grindelwald

1 HOUR

HARD

▶ ▶ ▶ Best time of year:
JUNE–OCTOBER

WEIGHT: 30–100 kg

EQUIPMENT: Gloves are useful

 ## Overview:

People have been enamored with flight for well over a century. We cannot think of a better way to capture the sense of freedom that comes with flying than by paragliding through the Swiss Alps. An adventure that could easily be added to any bucket list, paragliding is widely available in some of Switzerland's most celebrated locations.

In 1987, Verbier, Switzerland, hosted the inaugural, though not official, Paragliding World Championship. The event became official in 1989, when Austria hosted the first World Championships. Paragliding, as we know it today, has evolved through design and purpose over the years to become a popular recreational sport.

Children can participate with the consent of a parent/guardian but must weigh at least 30 kg. The maximum weight for paragliding is 100 kg. Please inform the company when booking if weights are close to either restriction.

Paragliding requires very little equipment: a licensed pilot, the chair harness, controls, the parachute (made of a series of fabric cells all tightly woven together), and good weather. To capitalize on the wind, the pilot starts from a nearby mountain or hillside. After a few steps, followed by a short run, the wind captures the sail, and you feel the euphoria as your feet gently leave the ground.

As a tandem experience, your pilot provides detailed instructions for a safe takeoff and helps you into your chair harness. Once airborne, witness the allure of the Swiss Alps from a fresh perspective, ride the thermals and glide through the air. During the 20-30 minute flight, time passes quickly because you're mesmerized by your surroundings. The pilot provides instructions for a safe landing in an open field.

 ## Tips:

- This is the greatest opportunity to experience flying! No skills or fitness levels are required.
- While paragliding requires minimal physical exertion, the level of bravery required may be high for some.
- The lift ticket to First is not included in the price of paragliding.
- Participants need to know where to meet their pilots. The meeting location may change due to weather and/or wind on any particular day. For this activity we review Grindelwald-First, where the meeting point is either at the lower lift station (Grindelwald) or at the top lift station (First).
- It's permissible to take a small, secured camera, but selfie sticks, phones, and cameras are not allowed.
- The pilot captures images of your flight, which are available for purchase.
- If the weather is less than ideal, show up early to potentially capitalize on a good weather window and/or establish the best take off location. Flights are cancelled if the weather is poor. Check the company's cancellation/rebooking policy.
- If you are prone to motion sickness, a daring flight is not for you. If you are a thrill seeker, let your pilot know.

 ## Contact Details:

Paragliding Jungfrau GmbH
Dorfstrasse 187
3818 Grindelwald
+41 79 77 99 000
tandem@pargliding-jungfrau.ch
paragliding-jungfrau.ch

A FLIGHT TO REMEMBER

More options:

+ Gstaad, BE
+ Interlaken, BE
+ Wengen, BE
+ Bad Ragaz, GR
+ Pontresina, GR
+ Weggis, LU
+ Engelberg, OW
+ Locarno, TI
+ Rivera, TI
+ Zermatt, VS

Whitewater Rafting

CANTON:
Bern

LOCATION:
Interlaken

START AND END POINT:
Interlaken

2.5 HOURS

MEDIUM

▶ ▶ ▶ Best time of year:

JUNE–SEPTEMBER

AGE RANGE:
8+

EQUIPMENT:
Swimsuit, towel, change of clothes

Overview:

For individuals, groups, or families new to rafting, whitewater rafting along the Lütschine River is a perfect excursion. We hired a guide from Outdoor Switzerland AG (an adventure company) to safely guide us down the river into Lake Brienz.

Your guide picks you up at a designated location and drives you to their center. At the center you will be provided with: wetsuits, life jackets, booties, and helmets. Then you're taken to the river entry point. Prior to launching the raft, you receive a thorough safety explanation. Then it's time to hit the water!

You paddle, laugh, learn about the area, and relax as you cruise down the river. Once in a safe location in Lake Brienz, jump in for a refreshing swim, then swim to shore to help your guide load the boat back onto the van.

Tips:

- This is a fabulous adventure for a group. There is a maximum of eight people per raft, plus the guide.
- Cellphones can be stored in a watertight container provided by your guide. Consider taking a waterproof camera.
- Pack some cash to purchase snacks or drinks at the end.
- There are varying levels of rafting offered. We chose the "Family Rafting" package as an introduction to the sport.
- Pick-up and drop-off service is available and must be selected at the time of booking.
- It's advisable to hire a company and/or guide that you feel comfortable with. We do not work with or receive any financial contributions from Outdoor Switzerland AG. While our guide was excellent, we cannot vouch for other guides or experiences provided by any company. Guides may be seasonally employed.
- If you're interested in a rafting experience without the need to hire a guide, consider rafting down the Aare River from Thun to Bern, BE. Rubber boats can be rented in Thun and returned in Bern. This is a long journey (roughly 28 km), so plan for a full day on the river. Life vests and barrels to store your cloths are provided by the company (aarebootsfahrten.ch).

 ## Contact Details:

Outdoor Switzerland AG
Hauptstrasse 15
3800 Matten bei Interlaken
+41 33 224 0707
info@outdoor.ch
outdoor.ch

More options:

+ **Simme River, in the Simmental, Därstetten, BE** (outdoor.ch)
+ **Rhine River, near Ilanz, GR** (wasserchraft.ch; swissriveradventures.ch; adventurebase.ch)
+ **Giarsun Gorge, Zuoz, GR** (engadinoutdoorcenter.ch)
+ **Vispa River, Visp, VS** (swissraft.ch; valrafting.com)
+ **Saane River, Chateau d'Oex, VD** (swissraft.ch)

The Valley of Waterfalls

CANTON:
Bern

LOCATION:
Lauterbrunnen

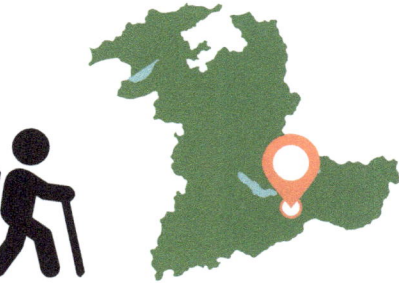

START AND END POINT:
Lauterbrunnen, Ey

3 HOURS

EASY

▶ ▶ ▶ Best time of year:
APRIL–SEPTEMBER

AGE RANGE:
5+

CHF

EQUIPMENT:
Warm, waterproof outdoor clothing, sturdy shoes

Overview:

Lauterbrunnen Valley is known as "the valley of waterfalls." With a whopping 72 stunning waterfalls, this must-see area is guaranteed to impress. It's a popular tourist destination, but don't let the crowds deter you! Pack a picnic lunch, find a shady spot and unwind. Beauty, such as that present in this valley, is meant to be savored.

The hike outlined, to Trümmelbach Falls, passes multiple waterfalls, including the impressive Staubbach Falls towering close to 300 m in height. This hike is ideal in the spring and summer months when the falls are at their prime. July is the peak of snowmelt.

Trümmelbach Falls, a UNESCO World Heritage Site, are a powerful, mind-blowing reminder of how intense nature can be. They're the biggest underground falls in Europe and pump an impressive 20,000 liters of water every second.

From the Lauterbrunnen, Ey bus stop, proceed uphill to the church that's just across the river. The trail begins on the other side of the parking lot. Follow signs toward Trümmelbachfälle. This path goes through the valley and across a field before crossing the river. Be careful crossing the road at the Trümmelbachfälle area. Return to Lauterbrunnen by following the path in reverse.

 ## Tips:

+ Check the website for opening hours.
+ There is an entry fee to access Trümmbelbach Falls.
+ Dogs and children aged four and under are not permitted to enter for safety reasons.
+ A small elevator is part of the tour and the falls are partially underground. If you're claustrophobic, this may not be the best excursion for you.
+ The waterfalls can be extremely loud and are unbelievably powerful. Keep children close.
+ A small kiosk and toilets are available onsite.

 ## Contact Details:

Familie Kaspar von Almen AG
Trümmelbach
3824 Stechelberg/Lauterbrunnen
+41 33 855 32 32
info@truemmelbachfaelle.ch
truemmelbachfaelle.ch

THE VALLEY OF WATERFALLS

More options:

+ Giessbach Falls near Brienz, BE
+ Oltschibachfall near Meiringen, BE
+ Berglistüber, Linthal, GL
+ Saut du Doubs, Les Brenets, NE
+ Dundelbach Falls, Lungern, OW
+ Thurwasserfälle, Alt St. Johann, SG
+ Cascata Piumogna, Faido, TI
+ Cascata di Foroglio, Cevio, TI
+ Stäubifall, Unterschächen, UR
+ Fellbach, Saas-Balen, VS
+ Chute de la Rèche, Grône, VS
+ Rhine Falls, Laufen-Uhwiesen, ZH

Swiss Bike Park Oberried

CANTON:
Bern

LOCATION:
Niederscherli

START AND END POINT:
Niederscherli, Oberried

2+ HOURS

MEDIUM

▶ ▶ ▶ Best time of year:
APRIL–OCTOBER

AGE RANGE:
4+

EQUIPMENT:
Gloves, helmet, padded bike shorts, back protection

Overview:

Opened in 2018, the park has a relaxed vibe and vast offerings: a children's track, practice areas, a pump track, trick jumps, uphill trails, downhill areas, a velodrome arena, rock garden, and technique areas. Courses and camps are offered for all levels.

This biker's paradise is meticulously designed with an emphasis on safety. Each area has an information board with tips from a professional in the discipline, QR codes for tutorials, and the emergency number to call and the site location should you require assistance.

With its impressive facilities and views to the Alps, this park provides an inclusive experience for people of all ages and abilities. There's truly something for everyone. Their goal is to create not only an amazing facility for bike lovers, but to also be a park for public recreation. We think they nailed it!

Have a look at their website beforehand to become familiar with the layout. There's a fabulous interactive map, plus a section that highlights their latest offers.

It's advised to arrive at the park by car; there's onsite parking. The nearest public transport stop is Thörishaus Dorf train station. A shuttle service is available from the train station: reserve via phone two days in advance.

 ## Tips:

+ Bring your own bike or rent one onsite. They also offer bikes to test ride for the different disciplines.
+ The park is open Monday to Saturday from 9:00–18:00, and on two Sundays per month.
+ To avoid crowds, consider visiting on a weekday.
+ The park's airbag section (for safely learning big jumps) is closed in bad weather.
+ Showers, toilets and a café are onsite, as well as a full-service bike shop.
+ Register in advance for all camps and courses.

 ## Contact Details:

Swiss Bike Park
Oberriedgässli 6
3145 Niederscherli
+41 31 848 22 12
info@swissbikepark.ch
swissbikepark.ch

More options:

- + Pumptrack Urnäsch, AR (pumptrack-urnaesch.ch)
- + Pumptrack Frutigen, BE (frutigresort.ch)
- + Bike Park Valbirse, BE (bikeparkvalbirse.ch)
- + Pumptrack Arosa, GR (arosa-bikeschool.ch)
- + Pumptrack Domat/Ems, GR (amedestrailhunters.ch)
- + Pumptrack Grenchen, SO (tissotvelodrome.ch)
- + Pumptrack Altendorf, SZ (altendorf.ch)
- + Kabi Bike Park, Oberiberg, SZ (bikeschulehochybrig.ch)
- + Pumptrack Schattdorf, UR (urbikers.ch)
- + Pumptrack Champéry, VS (regiondentsdumidi.ch)
- + Bike Park Zurich, ZH (bikeparkzuerich.ch)

Stand-up Paddleboarding (SUP)

CANTON: Fribourg
LOCATION: Lake Gruyère

START AND END POINT: Le Bry, Village

2+ HOURS

MEDIUM

▶ ▶ ▶ Best time of year:
JUNE–SEPTEMBER

AGE RANGE: 10+

EQUIPMENT: Swimsuit, hat, towel, sun protection

Overview:

Stand-up paddleboarding (SUP) made its debut as a sport in Hawaii, but people have been using paddles and rafts to navigate the water for thousands of years. Today, the sport has grown in popularity and for good reason: it's a fantastic way to experience bodies of water and a phenomenal workout.

Lake Gruyère is an artificial lake between Bulle and Fribourg. What makes this SUP experience unique is the opportunity to paddle out to the tiny Ogoz Island, which boasts a village dating back to the 13th century, including a castle and chapel where weddings are still conducted.

There aren't too many places in Switzerland that allow paddlers the opportunity to visit an island, so take full advantage of this experience during the summer months. (In mid- to late March, the lake is usually shallow enough to walk out to the island.)

 ## Tips:

- Paddleboards (including life vest and paddle) cost CHF 20 per hour or CHF 40 for a half-day rental. Canoes are also available.
- Paddleboarding requires balance and core strength, and it's recommended that you're a strong swimmer.
- Wearing a life vest is highly recommended. If you're more than 300 m from shore, you must have a flotation device with you.
- Keep your ankle leash on in the event you fall, or the wind blows you off your board.
- Use the buddy system whenever in the water and make sure others know where you are.
- Always be aware of your surroundings and oncoming watercrafts. Avoid marinas and busy harbors.
- For something different, moonlight paddleboarding is offered on Lake Zug in July and August, and SUP Yoga is available on the lakes of Zurich and Constance.

 ## Contact Details:

Canoës Gruyère
Pierre Vannier
+41 79 697 72 71
canoës-gruyère.ch

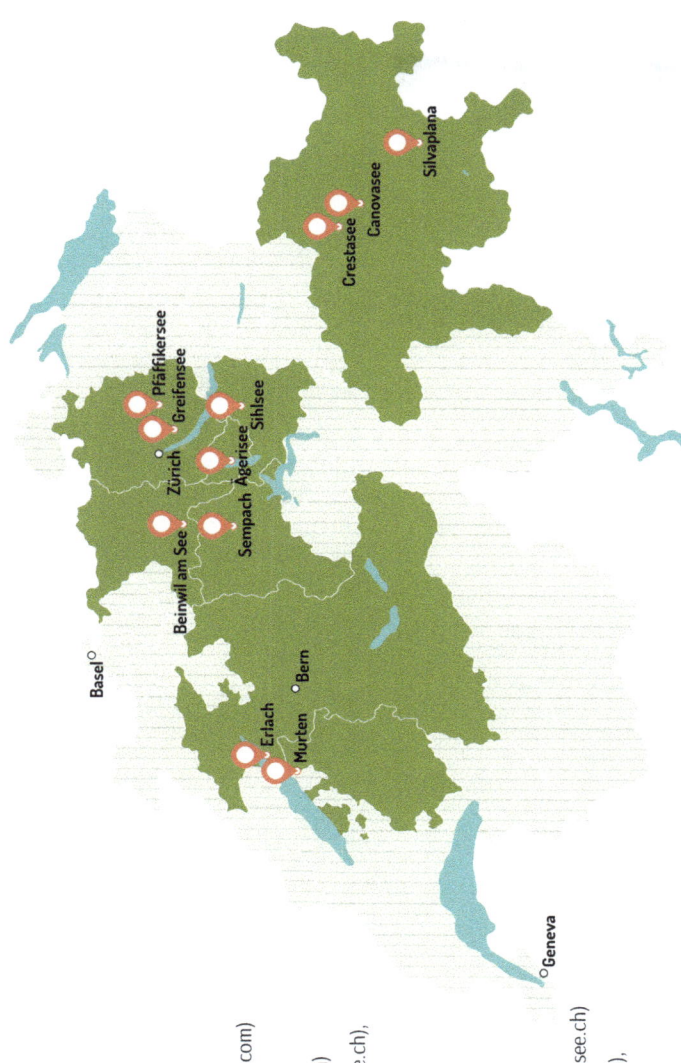

More options:

+ **Hallwilersee, AG: Beinwil am See** (strandbad-beinwilamsee.ch)
+ **Bielersee, BE: Erlach** (supstation.ch)
+ **Murtensee, FR: Murten** (bisenoire.ch)
+ **Canovasee, GR: Canovasee Badi** (canovasee.com)
+ **Crestasee, GR: Naturbad** (crestasee.com)
+ **Silvaplanersee, GR: Silvaplana** (kitesailing.ch)
+ **Sempachersee, LU: Nottwil** (caribbean-village.ch), **Sempach** (korporation-sempach.ch), **Schenkon** (seebadischenkon.ch)
+ **Sihlsee, SZ: Willerzell** (sihlsee-fisch.ch), **Sihlseebadi** (sihlseebadi.ch)
+ **Ägerisee, ZG: Oberägeri** (studenhuette.ch), **Unterägeri** (sup-aegerisee.ch)
+ **Greifensee, ZH: Strandbad Maur** (supgreifensee.ch)
+ **Pfäffikersee, ZH: Badi am See** (badiamsee.ch), **Strandbad Auslikon** (seekioskauslikon.ch)

Lake Murten Bike Tour

CANTON: Fribourg
LOCATION: Lake Murten

START AND END POINT: Murten

4+ HOURS

MEDIUM

▶ ▶ ▶ Best time of year:
APRIL–OCTOBER

AGE RANGE: 4+

EQUIPMENT: Bike gear, sunglasses

 ## Overview:

Switzerland is home to approximately 1500 lakes, which is a pretty impressive statistic for a tiny country. For a gorgeous biking path, consider the Lake Murten Route 480. This loop tour is a mix of road biking, forested trails and vineyard paths that provide commanding views of Lake Murten. Particularly lovely in the spring and autumn months, this route of about 30 km is full of rolling hills with ample opportunities for exploration.

From the train station, proceed down Freiburgstrasse; this starts you in a counterclockwise direction around Lake Murten following Route 480. Go through the roundabout and down the lower street (Ryf); signs point toward a boat dock and the town of Muntelier. Ryf turns into Hauptstrasse. After the large roundabout, the path turns left at the MB Metalbau building and continues through an industrial area. Soon, it's a tree-lined dirt path in a wildlife refuge.

The path deviates through the town of Sugiez and proceeds uphill to Mont Vully. Your first stop could be the Celtic Oppidum, perched high on the hill. For history buffs, this revived village that the Celts set on fire in 58 BC is worthy of a visit. After your break at Oppidum, drop down into the expansive vineyards before you come across the Mount Vully Caves (Les grottes des Roches Grises "La Lamberta"), a deviation (left) down the Route du Mont. This impressive cave system dates back to World War I and is a fantastic place of discovery for young and old. Weave in and out of the structure, taking in the nooks and crannies. This is the ideal location to appreciate a picnic lunch and to take a well-earned rest.

Hop back on your bikes and continue through the scenic vineyards. Continuing down Route du Mont, it merges with another road (Route du Quart Dessus) and meets up with the bike trail again. The path meanders through farms and fields to the quaint town of Vallamand-Dessus. The path soon drops back down toward the lake. The next point of interest is the bird estuary, on the southwest of the lake, near Faoug. From Faoug, Murten train station is approximately 5 km. Finish this picturesque route with a ride through (and stop in) this medieval town before returning your bikes and heading home.

 ## Tips:

- This bike tour is free if you arrive with your own bike and helmet.
- When renting a bike, the pick-up location is at Murten/Morat train station. Reserve your bikes and helmets in advance. Specify which type of bike you would like, if you require helmets, and the pick-up and return times. A discount is provided for Swiss Pass (SBB) cardholders.
- This diverse route is ideal for individuals with some biking experience.
- Murten celebrates SlowUp Murten at the end of April. This is a special day when the streets are closed to cars, and bikers have the opportunity to ride traffic-free from 10:00–17:00 (slowup.ch).
- The vineyards are in their prime during the autumn months, making this ride a feast for the eyes.
- During spring, the weather can still be cold and rather windy. You might like something to cover your ears.
- There aren't many toilets or water-refill spots along the route. Use the toilet at the train station and bring plenty of water.
- Some parts are on city streets but most is on exposed, open paths.
- Bring a first-aid kit and a small patch kit in the event of a flat tire.

 ## Contact Details:

Rent a Bike AG
+41 41 925 11 70
info@rentabike.ch
rentabike.ch

LAKE MURTEN BIKE TOUR

More options:

+ **Lungerersee Route 701 near Lungern, OW**
  (loop; 9 km)

+ **Pfäffikersee Route 210 near Pfäffikon, ZH**
  (loop; 12 km)

+ **Sarnersee Route 702 near Sarnen, OW**
  (loop; 18 km)

+ **Jura Route 7 from Basel to Nyon**
  (six stages; 280 km)

+ **Aare Route 8 from Oberwald (Gletsch) to Koblenz**
  (seven stages; 315 km)

+ **Rhône Route 1 from Andermatt to Geneva**
  (eight stages; 350 km)

+ **Mittlelland Route 5 from Romanshorn to Lausanne**
  (seven stages; 375 km)

+ **Rhine Route 2 from Andermatt to Basel**
  (nine states; 435 km)

+ **Lakes Route 9 from Montreaux to Rorschach**
  (10 stages; 510 km)

+ **Herzen Route 99 from Lausanne to Rorschach**
  (13 stages; 725 km)

Mountain Scooters

□ **CANTON:**
Graubünden

○ **LOCATION:**
Chur

START AND END POINT:
Brambrüesch

2-3 HOURS

EASY

▶ ▶ ▶ Best time of year:

JUNE–OCTOBER

AGE RANGE:
6+

EQUIPMENT:
Sturdy shoes, gloves
(in cool weather)

MOUNTAIN SCOOTERS

Overview:

High above Chur sits the sleepy mountain area of Brambrüesch. Void of crowds, this petite mountain is perfect for a day of adventure! Catch the 16-minute gondola from Chur up to Brambrüesch.

If you're new to the world of mountain scooters, allow us a moment to indulge you. Take a bike, remove the seat, add a platform to stand on, and replace the wheels with two robust mountain tires ... the mountain scooter is born! You'll actually see many variations of mountain scooters: some are on three wheels, low to the ground, and some have been pimped out for downright crazy rides.

This 5 km route from Brambrüesch (AIS Sports School Brambus Center) to Känzeli is the ultimate way to make your way down the mountain. The path is wide with a gradual descent and the views are impressive. For first-time scooter riders, this is a fabulous place! And to help you get started, every run starts with a two-minute overview/explanation from the staff.

If you want to up your scooter game, Brambrüesch also offers mountain boarding, which is essentially a "mountain skateboard" with a handbrake. If you long for more in the way of adventure, the area also offers "dirt surfing," which creates the feeling of snowboarding during summer.

 ## Tips:

+ Open Tuesday to Sunday. Check the opening hours on the website.
+ Activities start from the AIS Sports School Brambus Center, which is roughly a 15-minute walk from the Brambrüesch gondola station.
+ Helmets are provided at the time of scooter rental and are included in the fee.
+ Children must be 10 years of age to ride a scooter alone; if younger than 10, they can ride with a parent.
+ The AIS Sports School offers a variety of summer and winter sports training courses.

 ## Contact Details:

AIS Sportschule
Brambus Center
Riedboda
7074 Malix
+41 81 250 19 46
info@ais-sportschule.ch
ais-sportschule.ch

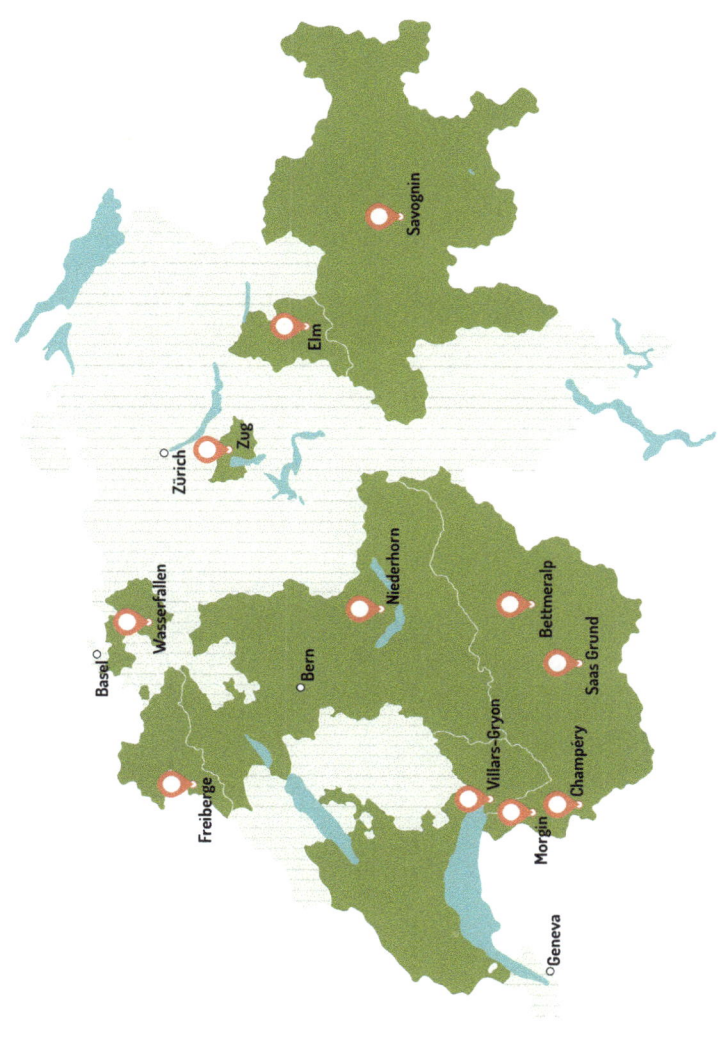

More options:

- **Niederhorn, BE** (niederhorn.ch)
- **Wasserfallen, BL** (region-wasserfallen.ch)
- **Elm, GL** (sportbahnenelm.ch)
- **Savognin, GR** (valsurses.ch)
- **Freiberge, JU** (j3l.ch)
- **Saas Grund, VS** (saas-fee.ch)
- **Bettmeralp, VS** (aletscharena.ch)
- **Champéry, VS** (regiondentsdumidi.ch)
- **Morgin, VS** (regiondentsdumidi.ch)
- **Villars-Gryon, VD** (alpesvaudoises.ch)
- **Zug, ZG** (trottiplausch-zug.ch)

Cross Golf Brambrüesch

CANTON: Graubünden
LOCATION: Chur

START AND END POINT: Brambrüesch

2-3 HOURS

EASY

▶ ▶ ▶ Best time of year:
JULY–OCTOBER

AGE RANGE: 6+

EQUIPMENT: Comfortable shoes

Overview:

While traditional golf courses are pricey and a bit rigid when it comes to rules, clothing, and guidelines, Cross Golf is anything but: it's simple, accessible, and fabulous outdoor recreation.

A game very similar to golf, Cross Golf requires that players use just one club and a single ball over nine holes. There are no standard greens, simply holes or targets placed in a stunning Alpine setting. The object of the game is simple: who can get their ball in the hole or target with the least number of strokes?

Cross Golf is a fantastic introduction to golf for people of all ages and abilities. If you are new to golf, don't worry! No prior skills or natural talent are required. This is the ultimate game for novices and groups! For a new take on traditional golf and/or Cross Golf, consider the Urban-Golf Parcours located in Winterthur (winterthur.com).

Catch the gondola from Chur up to Brambrüesch. The Cross Golf course is just across from the gondola station.

Tips:

- The course is open daily from July to October. Check the website for exact dates as they change each year.
- Purchase a gondola and golf "combi ticket" at the gondola station in Chur. Adults cost CHF 35/28 (without/with Half Fare Card or GA) and children cost CHF 17. You must pay a deposit of CHF 10 for each ball. Watch your ball carefully in the tall grass, as balls are easy to lose!
- Collect the Cross Golf equipment (club, ball and tee) from inside the Brambrüesch gondola station.
- Cross Golf balls are softer than normal golf balls.
- Groups of 10 or more must register in advance by using an online booking form.
- Use caution with your balls and tees around the grazing cows in the area!

Contact Details:

Chur Tourism
Bahnhofplatz 3
Postfach 115
7000 Chur
+41 81 252 18 18
info@churtourismus.ch
chur.graubuenden.ch

CROSS GOLF BRAMBRÜESCH

More options:

Cross Golf and Swin Golf, though not synonymous, are very similar. Here, we provided Swin Golf options for further exploration.

+ Swin Golf Tschugg, BE
+ Swin Golf Neuchâtel, NE
+ Swin Golf Hochwald, SO
+ Swin Golf Nax, VS
+ Swin Golf Cremin, VD

The Longest Toboggan Ride

CANTON: Graubünden
LOCATION: Churwalden

START AND END POINT: Bergbahnen

30+ MINUTES

EASY

▶ ▶ ▶ Best time of year:
MAY–OCTOBER

AGE RANGE: 3+ with a parent

EQUIPMENT: Weather-appropriate clothing

Overview:

Known in German-speaking Switzerland as *Rodelbahn*, these downhill, metal Alpine toboggan runs attract people of all ages. You sit in a specially designed cart attached to a long metal tube or rails. The experience can be fast; luckily, there are handbrakes and seatbelts!

For the longest toboggan run in Switzerland (and a Guinness World Records holder), make your way to the Pradaschier Rodelbahn in Churwalden for a thrilling ride.

From the Churwalden, Bergbahnen bus stop, follow signs toward Pradaschier along Girabodawäg. There is a large parking lot at the end of Girabodawäg. The ticket kiosk is located on the other side of the parking lot. There are two lifts: the one on the left takes you to Heidbüel (hiking opportunities await) and the one on the right takes you to the top of the Pradaschier toboggan run. Inquire about the Family Card, which provides a discount. The lift also accepts the Half Fare Card and GA.

There's a great view of the track from the chairlift on your way up the mountain. This toboggan runs has 31 turns, a height difference of just under 500 m, and is just over 3 km long. The duration of the ride is quick, lasting only about seven minutes, but those minutes are unforgettable.

The Pradaschier Rodelbahn is also special because it's open in both summer and winter. Others tend to only be open during summer.

Tips:

+ Children (up to their sixth birthday) ride for free! That's awesome!
+ Children can ride alone from the age of eight. Children from three to seven years old must ride with an adult.
+ The toboggan run is open daily from 9:30–17:00. From early July to late August the course opens at 9:00.
+ From May to October, if you visit before 11:00 you get the "Early Bird" special, which consists of two rides for the price of one.
+ Pregnant women and people with medical conditions are not permitted to ride.
+ The toboggan run is closed in bad weather, for safety reasons.
+ For additional fun, the area is home to a 1.7 km-long zipline! Opening times are the same.

Contact Details:

Pradaschier. Der Erlebnisberg
Girabodawäg 16
7075 Churwalden
T +41 81 356 21 80
info@pradaschier.ch
pradaschier.ch

THE LONGEST TOBOGGAN RIDE

More options:

- **Jakobsbad, AI** (kronberg.ch)
- **Langenbruck, BL** (deinkick.ch)
- **Grindelwald, BE** (pfingstegg.ch)
- **Kandersteg, BE** (oeschinensee.ch)
- **Davos, GR** (schatzalp.ch)
- **Schongau, LU** (schongiland.ch)
- **Sörenberg, LU** (soerenberg.ch)
- **Wirzweli, NW** (wirzweli.ch)
- **Engelberg, OW** (brunni.ch)
- **Flumserberg, SG** (floomzer.ch)
- **Goldingen, SG** (atzmaennig.ch)
- **Sattel-Hockstuckli, SZ** (sattel-hochstuckli.ch)
- **Rivera, TI** (montetamaro.ch)
- **Saas-Fee, VS** (feeblitz.ch)
- **Les Diablerets, VD** (glacier3000.ch)

Guided Ibex and Marmot Tour

CANTON:
Graubünden

LOCATION:
Pontresina

START AND END POINT:
Alp Languard

5+ HOURS

MEDIUM

▶ ▶ ▶ Best time of year:
JUNE–OCTOBER

AGE RANGE:
10+

EQUIPMENT:
Hiking shoes, sun protection, layered clothing

 ## Overview:

Pontresina is known as an ibex paradise, and for good reason: it's home to one of Switzerland's largest ibex colonies. Affectionately known as "king of the Alps," ibex are the focal point of this area, which includes an ibex playground, gorgeous hiking trails and free guided tours. We recommend it be high on your "must visit" list.

Book your tour in advance and meet your guide at 9:00 at the Alp Languard chairlift in Pontresina. Be prepared for a long day of hiking, searching, observing, picnicking, and marveling at the stunning landscape. Your guide knows where to look for the animals high on the mountains and, if luck prevails, you'll spot ibex and/or marmots.

The educational element of the tour is spectacular. The guide provides detailed information regarding the daily lives of ibex, how they endure the harsh winters and terrain, and what happens when they become ill. You'll also learn about marmots and their natural habitats.

Overall, the tour is ideal for those who wish to learn more about the Pontresina region and its native plants and animals.

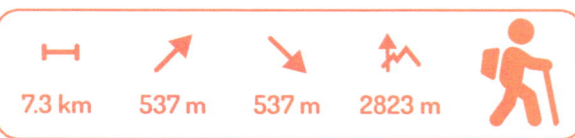

 ## Tips:

- This tour (available only in German) is free! You are, however, responsible for your chairlift tickets. You start in the valley with your guide and return down via chairlift at the end of the day.
- The group size is intentionally small. You must register in advance to book tickets (engadin.ch).
- Bring binoculars if you have them: the chance to spot animals in their natural habitat is a genuine thrill.
- The route distance is an estimate, based on our experience. The route may vary depending on the guide.
- Hunting season begins September 30. This is not a danger for hikers but may make the ibex harder to spot.
- Bring your own lunch, water (there are no opportunities to fill along the way) and snacks.
- Toilets are available at the lift station only.
- This is a long day out with a relatively robust hike. Plan accordingly.
- There is an estimated altitude change of 600 m on this route.

 ## Contact Details:

Pontresina Tourismus
Via Maistra 133
7504 Pontresina
+41 81 838 83 20
info@pontresina.ch
pontresina.ch

GUIDED IBEX AND MARMOT TOUR

More options:

+ Diemtigtal (snails), Diemtigen, BE
+ Schwendi Brönd Wildlife (deer), Habkern, BE
+ Wildlife tour, Niederhorn, BE
+ Payerne et Région (beavers), Estavayer-le-Lac, FR
+ Birds of Prey, Bergün, GR
+ Wildlife watching (deer), Val Roseg, GR
+ Pilatus Kulm (ibex), Kreins, LU
+ Creux du Van (ibex, chamois), Noiraigue, NE
+ Rheintal (birds), Altstätten, SG
+ Selzach (stork colony), SO
+ Wildlife tour (ibex, chamois), Göscheneralp, UR
+ Birkendorf Bürchen (squirrels), Bürchen, VS
+ Val d'Hérens (deer), Hérémence, VS

Alpine Mountain Bike Tour

CANTON:
Graubünden

LOCATION:
St. Moritz

START POINT:
St. Moritz

END POINT:
Scuol-Tarasp

3 DAYS

HARD

▶ ▶ ▶ Best time of year:

JUNE–OCTOBER

AGE RANGE:

16+

EQUIPMENT:

Bike gear, hydration pack, layered clothing

Overview:

Graubünden is a mountain biking haven and many hotels and mountain inns are happy to accommodate riders. This tour takes you through several remote areas, heading over the Bernina Pass and through the high Val Mora. Couple this with two restful nights and delicious food, the tour makes for a great balance: a wild Alpine escape with warm hospitality.

Longer mountain biking journeys are less about the destination and more about the experience. When you ride for three consecutive days, things rarely transpire as planned and that's when the real adventure begins. This route is long and takes you through out-of-the-way areas, but you're never too far from civilization.

DAY 1:
45.1 km | 5 h | 1303 m | 1257 m

From the St. Moritz train station, follow the red signposts with the bicycle symbol in the direction of Pontresina (heading east out of St. Moritz). The trail continues southeast toward Lago Bianco and up to the Bernina Pass (Ospizio Bernina), the highest point on the tour. Continue over the pass, where the sparse landscape clears your mind until the downhill route to Livigno awakens the senses. Do not miss the left turn toward Livigno! This is the only road from this direction to get there.

DAY 2:
54.5 km | 6 h | 1516 m | 2339 m

From Livigno, continue north, turning right before Lago di Livigno. This puts you on the trail on the right side when looking north. Continue up the Alpisella Valley in the direction of Val Mora, a remote and quiet Swiss valley on the edge of Italy. After coming down from Val Mora, follow Route 32 toward Malles Venosta. This connects with Müstair. Consider stopping at the Convent of St. John in Müstair. A UNESCO World Heritage Site since 1983, it contains some of the best-preserved frescos dating back to the Middle

Ages. Additionally, down the road in Tubre, Italy, the Church of San Giovanni has one of the oldest-known frescos of St. Christopher from the early 13th century. From Müstair (the easternmost village in Switzerland), head toward the Italian border and on to Malles Venosta (alternatively, you can follow Route 1 to Tschierv, but this will deviate from the tour. Route 1 can also be taken to Scuol the next day).

DAY 3:

64.9 km | 7 h | 3464 m | 3174 m

The longest day, so plan to leave early. It's a slow climb into Austria and renowned for headwinds. From Malles Venosta, ride north toward Nauders then follow the road to the left for Route 443, where you pass several small lakes and a larger lake. Take a break for coffee and pastry in Nauders before descending back into Switzerland on your way to Scuol.

TOTAL:

164.4 km | 6283 m | 6770 m | 2327 m

ALPINE MOUNTAIN BIKE TOUR

Tips:

- This tour overlaps part of the Alpine Bike Route 1 and a small part of the Trans-Altarezia Route 32. If you have more time, consider riding this route in reverse, and extending your journey along Route 1 to Bivio, crossing over the Septimer Pass where Roman roads are still visible! Route 1 is 670 km from Scuol to Leysin (schweizmobil.ch).
- This route zigzags the Swiss border and crosses into Italy and Austria. Bring the necessary travel documents, your Rega card, and Euros.
- Pausing at the Convent of St. John in Müstair might just feel like a spiritual experience. It's been a stopping point for many over the centuries, starting with Charlemagne, as legend has it.
- Overnight stays in Livigno and Malles Venosta are the best locations for this tour.
- As this tour takes place over multiple days, it may be difficult to mountain bike with a full backpack, particularly downhill. Consider booking longer tours with an organized group that offers gear transport between locations.
- If you choose to ride this route during the autumn months, be aware that there can be snowfall on the passes.
- There is a bus service from Livigno in Italy to Punt la Drossa in Switzerland which bypasses the Val Mora if snow is present. You can connect to Müstair via the road over Pass dal Fuorn.
- It is not recommended to ride over the Schlinigpass (Malles Venosta in Italy to Scuol in Switzerland) and down through the Uina Valley. This route is extremely dangerous. If you wish to see this area, consider a planned hiking trip at a later date.

Contact Details:

Hotel Touring Livigno
Via Plan 117
23030 Livigno, Italy
+39 0342 996131
info@touringlivigno.com
touringlivigno.com

Hotel Greif
Via Generale Ignaz Verdross 40
39024 Malles Venosta, Italy
+39 0473 831189
info@hotel-greif.com
hotel-greif.com

More options:

+ **Eiger Bike-Challenge in Grindelwald, BE** (20–80 km, including a children's race)
+ **Arosa Lenzerheide Tour Route 634 from Arosa, GR** (55 km loop)
+ **Scalettapass/Keschhütte Route 339 from Davos-Platz, GR** (71 km loop)
+ **Rheinschluchttour Route 260 from Ilanz, GR** (one or two stages; 87 km loop)
+ **Swiss Bike Masters Route 333 from Küblis, GR** (four stages; 115 km loop)
+ **Gottardo Bike Route 65 from Andermatt, UR, to Biasca, TI** (three stages; 110 km)
+ **Valais Alpine Bike Route 41 from Crans-Montana, VS, to Sierre, VS** (six stages; 200 km)

Camping in the Trees

CANTON: Lucerne
LOCATION: Pilatus

START AND END POINT: Fräkmüntegg

1+ NIGHT

MEDIUM

▶ ▶ ▶ Best time of year:
JUNE–SEPTEMBER

AGE RANGE: 5+

EQUIPMENT: Sleeping bag, toiletries, headlamp, bug spray

Overview:

Camping is the ultimate adventure but when your tent is suspended between trees in an enchanted forest, the experience becomes even more exciting. If you're looking for an exceptional opportunity for families and groups, head to the Pilatus region.

With each booking, you receive round-trip lift tickets from Kriens–Fräkmüntegg–Kriens, access to the rope park from 17:00–20:00, dinner in Restaurant Fräkmüntegg, your overnight in the tree tent, plus breakfast in the morning. A ride on the Dragon Glider is a slow, meandering flight through the trees from Fräkmüntegg to Drachenalp and is also included with the overnight stay.

The magic of this overnight adventure comes to life when the visitors retreat down the mountain at the end of the day. Once the crowds dissipate, the mountain becomes a sanctuary of calm. It's rare to have a mountain to yourself for the night.

While at the top, don't forget to take in the sunset. As the sun slowly fades, the mountain sings you to sleep with the sounds of cowbells in the distance and wind in the trees. You feel fully relaxed in your suspended tent as sleep washes over you.

Tips:

- This totally unique experience is offered from June to August.
- Advance reservations are required.
- Have your printed reservation with you as the QR code is your lift pass. The ride is included in your overnight stay.
- Bring your own sleeping bags. Everything else is provided.
- Each tent sleeps a maximum of three people.
- Dinner is served in the restaurant at 20:00.
- It's perfect for those new to camping, as very few supplies are required.
- If you're looking for additional activities in the area, head over to Pilatus Kulm. Situated at 2132 m, this location offers stunning views of the surrounding area and plenty of hiking, theme, and running trails. Half Fare and Junior cards are accepted on Pilatus Kulm.

Contact Details:

Pilatus-Bahnen AG
Schlossweg 1
6010 Kriens
Tel: +41 41 329 11 11
info@pilatus.ch
pilatus.ch

CAMPING IN THE TREES

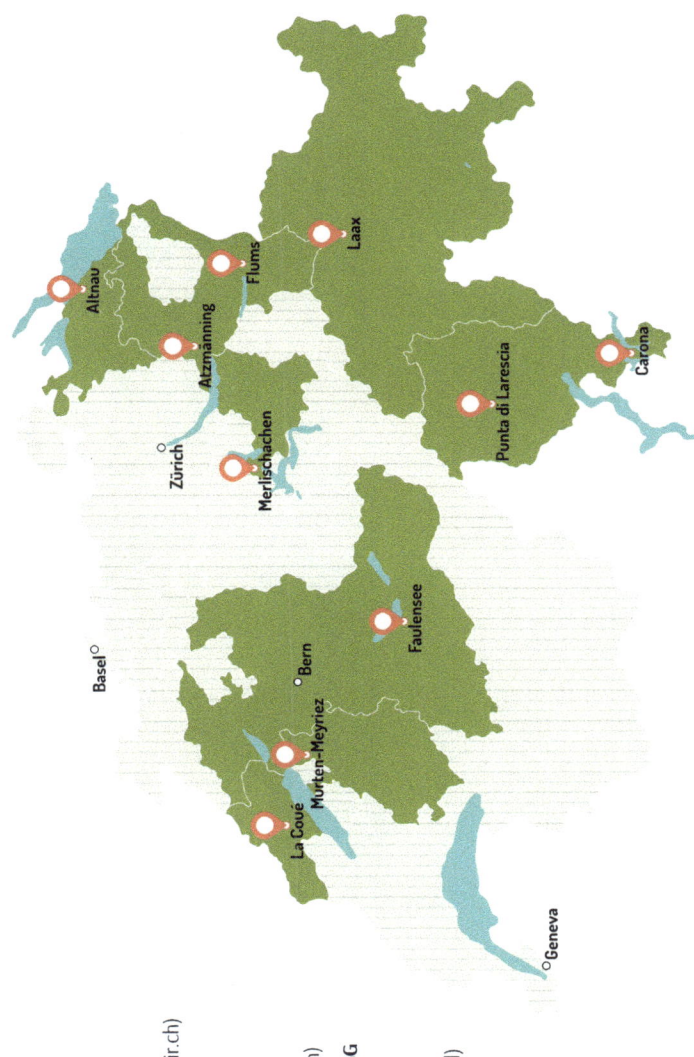

More options:

+ **Sealander floating hotel, Faulensee, BE** (interlaken.ch)
+ **Tree house, Murten-Meyriez, FR** (vieuxmanoir.ch)
+ **TCS Pop-Up Glamping Village, Laax, GR** (tcs-glamping.ch)
+ **Tree glamping, La Coué, NE** (lacoue.ch)
+ **POD houses, Atzmännig, SG** (atzmaennig.ch)
+ **Tree tents, Baumzelt am Kleinberg, Flums, SG** (nomady.ch)
+ **Yurts, Merlischachen, SZ** (gehren.ch)
+ **Bubble-Hotels, Altnau, TG** (himmelbett.cloud)
+ **Tree tents, Hotel Villa Carona, Carona, TI** (villacarona.ch)
+ **Under the Stars, Capanna Gorda, Punta di Larescia, TI** (capannagorda-sanda.ch)

Bringing the Cows Up and Down the Mountains

CANTON:
Obwalden

LOCATION:
Engelberg

START AND END POINT:

Kloster

2+ HOURS

EASY

▶ ▶ ▶ Best time of year:

SEPTEMBER–OCTOBER

AGE RANGE:

ALL AGES

EQUIPMENT:

Sun protection, sturdy shoes

Overview:

Once the summer months arrive, farmers or herdsmen and women take their cows to higher Alpine pastures to let them graze on grass, herbs and wildflowers. This special occasion is known as Alpaufzug in German-speaking Switzerland. The trek is demanding, but the cows are guided up carefully.

Then, when summer ends and the weather turns cold, the cows, and other animals including sheep and goats, make the descent to lower pastures and the warmth of their barns. Bringing the cattle down is celebrated throughout Switzerland and is known as "Alpabzug" in German-speaking Switzerland. Farmers dress in regional clothing and the cows are adorned with flowers. The crowd goes wild, ringing cowbells and waving flags.

Gather family and friends, select your location (there are multiple locations and dates throughout Switzerland) and get ready for this festive and traditional Swiss experience! Each village is rich with unique traditions that mark this special time. Markets offer homemade goods, regional products, and traditional Swiss food such as sausages, raclette, local cheese and crepes. Music, games and drinks during the Alpabzug are quite common and, if you're lucky, you might be able to vote for the most beautiful cow.

While in Engelberg, visit the local Benedictine monastery, which dates back to 1120 and is home to about 30 monks. Book a tour in German, French, English or Italian and allow 1–2 hours to learn the detailed history of this magnificent location. Afterward, visit their onsite dairy and watch the creamy milk turn into delicious cheese. The dairy and shop are open daily from 9:30–15:30.

 ## Tips:

+ For the exact date, start time and route each year: engelberg.ch
+ The procession usually runs along parts of Engelberg's main street, Dorfstrasse.
+ The event takes place in all weather.
+ The cows are typically well behaved, but may get nervous in crowds. Be aware.

Contact Details:

Engelberg-Titlis Tourismus AG
Hinterdorfstrasse 1
6390 Engelberg
+41 41 639 77 77
welcome@engelberg.ch
engelberg.ch

BRINGING THE COWS UP AND DOWN THE MOUNTAINS

More options:

- Engstligenalp BE
- Innertkirchen, BE
- Albeuve, FR
- Charmey, FR
- Jaun, FR
- Brigels, GR
- Müstair, GR
- Einsiedeln, SZ
- Ayer, VS
- La Fouly, VS
- L'Etivaz, VD
- St-Cergue, VD

Balmberg Rope Park

CANTON: Solothurn
LOCATION: Balmberg

START AND END POINT: Oberbalmber, Kurhaus

3 HOURS

MEDIUM

▶ ▶ ▶ Best time of year:

APRIL–NOVEMBER

AGE RANGE:

4+

EQUIPMENT:

Long pants, sturdy shoes

BALMBERG ROPE PARK

Overview:

Rope parks are a tremendous way to test your balance, agility, and strength. The beautifully maintained rope park at Balmberg is nestled deep in the woods and provides shade on hot days. The park consists of 10 unique courses, offering opportunities for all skill levels.

The entrance is located approximately 200 m up the hill from the Oberbalmberg, Kurhaus bus stop. If you plan to arrive by car, there is a large parking lot onsite. We recommend you drive from the Solothurn side, as the other approach is on narrow roads (but if you appreciate wild drives, go for it!).

A safety class is required before starting your climbing experience. The knowledgeable staff take the time to instruct you on how to safely navigate the courses. The park offers ziplines, free falls, 186 platforms and routes for beginners to experts. The options are endless and ensure a full day of activity.

Start out slowly, to assess your skill and comfort levels, as you traverse your way through the courses. Climb through trees, over bridges, and practice your steadiness and perseverance as you go. The rope park provides a mental and physical challenge for all participants. Don't be surprised if you're exhausted at the end of the day!

Oh, and remember, rope parks are great team builders for groups or companies. You cheer for each other during challenging moments and give hearty high-fives when a course is complete.

Tips:

+ **The park is open daily (including public holidays) from 9:00–18:00.**
+ **Helmets, gloves and climbing harnesses are provided.**
+ **For each ticket purchased, you're permitted to climb for a maximum of three hours. At that time, your equipment must be returned.**
+ **The park is large enough to accommodate more than 200 climbers.**
+ **The park remains open in rain, but closes for thunderstorms and/or heavy winds.**
+ **Long pants are advised at rope parks to avoid rope burns on the legs.**
+ **Lockers, toilets, picnic tables and barbecue stations are available onsite.**
+ **Groups of more than 10 need to reserve in advance.**
+ **Comprehensive list of Swiss rope parks: seilparks.ch**

 ## Contact Details:

Rope Park Balmberg
Oberbalmberg 25
4524 Balmberg
+41 32 637 14 14
seilpark-balmberg.ch

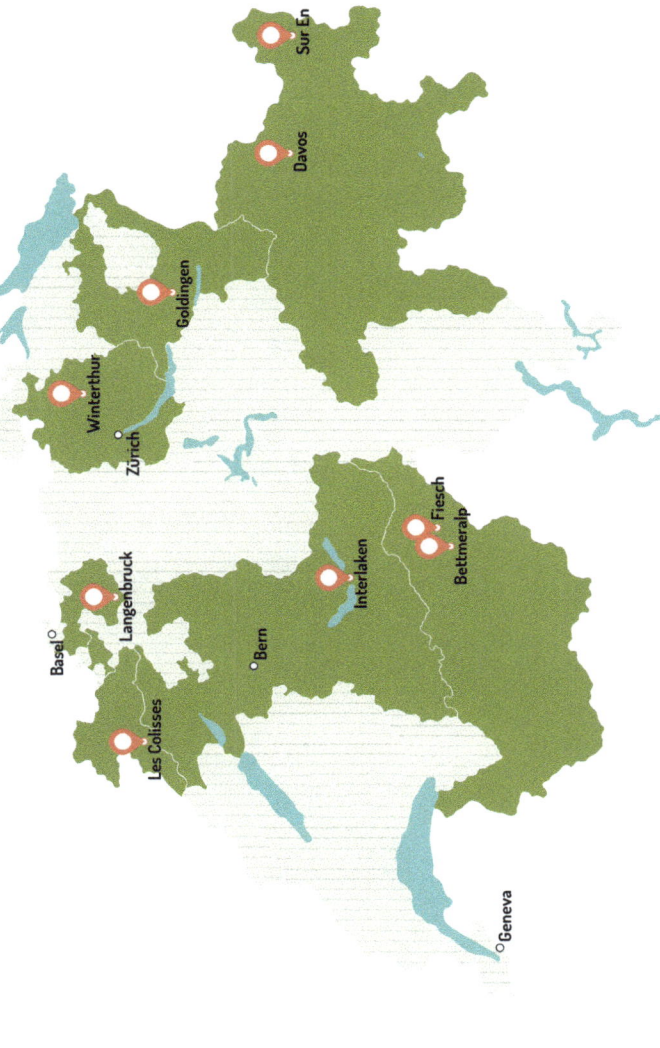

More options:

+ Seilpark Langenbruck, BL
+ Outdoor Seilpark Interlaken, BE
+ Davos Adventure Park, GR
+ Seilpark Engadin, Sur En, GR
+ Forest Jump, Les Colisses, JU
+ Seilpark Atzmännig, Goldingen, SG
+ Seilpark Baschweri, Bettmeralp, VS
+ Swiss Seilpark, Fiesch, VS
+ Seilpark Winterthur, ZH

A Hidden Past

CANTON: Ticino

LOCATION: St. Gotthard Pass

START AND END POINT: Gotthard, Passhöhe

1–2 HOURS

EASY

▶ ▶ ▶ Best time of year:

JUNE–OCTOBER

AGE RANGE: 4+

EQUIPMENT: Warm clothes, sturdy shoes

 ## Overview:

As part of Switzerland's defensive system against foreign invasion, the government mapped out a plan known as the National Redoubt (*Schweizer Réduit*) that led to construction of bunkers, fortifications, and barricades across the nation. Leading up to and during World War II, the construction increased to including multiple hidden mountain locations. During that time, thankfully, Operation Tannenbaum, a World War II invasion plan of Switzerland, was never enacted.

The main intent of the National Redoubt was to slow down an advancing invader and secure the mountain region by denying access over (and through) the Alps. There are several locations where these defensive structures were built to look like farmhouses and regular buildings. Today, many of these have been declassified and offer tours to show visitors what it was like during perilous times.

One of Switzerland's largest fortifications, Sasso San Gottardo, is at the top of St. Gotthard Pass. This extensive network of tunnels, armaments, facilities, and railway supply lines created a bird's-eye view over both sides of the pass for the Swiss military. The large cannons hidden inside were capable of targeting distances over 23 km away!

This impressive tour guides you through the interior of the Alps. If you're interested in history or just curious about what lies beneath the surface of Switzerland, this is a great experience.

From the Gotthard Passhöhe bus stop, follow the cobblestone road around the righthand side of the small lake toward the entrance of the Sasso San Gottardo. If travelling by car, drive down Tremola Road (the old St. Gotthard Pass) to Airolo. With its cobblestones and multiple turns, you might need a break to enjoy the views! Heading the other direction, consider stopping at the Devil's Bridge (Teufelsbrücke) to the north of Andermatt on your way toward Lucerne.

Tips:

- Due to the location, St. Gotthard Pass is only open from June to October.
- The bus service from Andermatt or Airolo may not be available at the beginning of June.
- Pay an additional fee for a guided or extended tour which covers more areas within the fortress. Some tours require a minimum of eight people.
- Sasso San Gottardo hosts various exhibitions. Check the website for what's currently on show.
- Temperatures inside the fortress range between 6–18°C
- Parking in front of the fortress is free of charge while visiting.
- Pets are not allowed inside the fortress.
- Pay attention to the required travel time and be aware of the opening times. When driving over the passes in the area, it may take more time than the GPS indicates.

Contact Details:

Fondazione Sasso San Gottardo
Via della Stazione 4
6780 Airolo
+41 84 411 66 00
info@sasso-sangottardo.ch
sasso-sangottardo.ch

More options:

+ **Military and Fortress Museum Reuenthal, Full-Reuenthal, AG** (festungsmuseum.ch)
+ **Hauenstein Fortification, Langenbruck, BL** (fortifikation-hauenstein.ch)
+ **Fischbalmen Beatenbucht Bunker, Sigriswil, BE** (bunker-fischbalmen.ch)
+ **Fortress Vitznau, LU** (festung-vitznau.ch)
+ **Fortress Albula, Bergün, GR** (festung-albula.ch)
+ **Fortress Museum Crestawald, Sufers, GR** (crestawald.ch)
+ **Sonnenberg Civilian Bunker, Kriens, LU** (unterirdisch-ueberleben.ch)
+ **Fortress Mondascia, Biasca, TI** (fortemondascia.ch)
+ **Simplon Fortress Naters, VS** (simplonfestungnaters.ch)
+ **Fortress St. Maurice, Saint-Maurice, VS** (forteresse-st-maurice.ch)

Via Ferrata Diavolo

CANTON:
Uri

LOCATION:
Andermatt

START AND END POINT:
Andermatt

3–5 HOURS

HARD

▶ ▶ ▶ Best time of year:
JUNE–OCTOBER

AGE RANGE:
14+

EQUIPMENT:
Hiking shoes, via ferrata set

Overview:

The term via ferrata means iron path in Italian. These climbing routes throughout the Alps consist of fixed handholds, metal cables, and sometimes ladders and footholds. Physically and mentally demanding, there are roughly 35 via ferratas scattered across this tiny country.

Taking on a via ferrata is a fabulous adventure, but not for the faint of heart! Via ferratas are ideal for thrill-seekers but should only be attempted by those with climbing knowledge, mental fortitude, and physical strength. The Via Ferrata Diavolo is listed as a K2 (K1 being easy and K6 extremely difficult), making it the ultimate route for those new to the sport, though skill is still required.

This scenic climb, with the Reuss River and Devil's Bridge below, starts at 1400 m and finishes at approximately 1850 m.

Starting from Andermatt train station, follow Bahnhofstrasse to Gotthardstrasse and turn left, following the signs toward Teufelsbrücke. This eventually leads you along the Reuss River. Near the roundabout, stop at Imholz Sport Piazza Gottardo store, in the courtyard on the other side of the Radison Blu Hotel, if you need to rent equipment.

The path to the via ferrata continues down Gotthardstrasse, crossing the road several times before arriving at the Teufelsbrücke. You should see signs, just past Restaurant Teufelsbrücke, for the via ferrata. Clip in at the start before scaling the rock face using the handholds and foot rungs. The views from the granite wall of the Schöllenen Gorge are impressive.

Though demanding, there are locations to rest along the route. Once safely at the top, enjoy the scenery before hiking the via ferrata exit trail. The exit is on an Alpine (White-Blue-White) route which then connects to the main hiking trail for the approximate 3.6 km descent to Andermatt. This places you at the base of the lift station across from Andermatt train station. If you prefer to take the lift down, it's approximately 2.4 km to the Nätschen lift station from the via ferrata exit path.

A via ferrata should never be attempted without general climbing knowledge. In addition, we highly recommend taking a course with a trained professional to familiarize yourself with the equipment, required skills, and heights. Rope parks can also be good starting points. If you are new and wish to climb a via ferrata, it's advised to hire a trained guide. Inquire about a guide at local tourist offices or sports shops. Start at a K1/K2 level when beginning. Please never underestimate the skill or fitness required to participate in a via ferrata.

VIA FERRATA DIAVOLO

 ## Tips:

- Bring your own or rent equipment (harness, via ferrata set, helmet, and gloves). The cost of this adventure depends on the amount of equipment you need.
- Never attempt this route in wet or inclement weather.
- Take your time and always ensure that your carabiners are properly secured!
- Between December and April, the Via Ferrata Diavolo is in a protected wildlife area and should not be used.
- A military via ferrata is located 200 m from the Via Ferrata Diavolo start. It's not permitted to climb on the military via ferrata, which is used for training purposes.
- Search "grading systems" to view the via ferrata scale of difficulty and "safety on via ferrata" for important tips on the Schweizer Alpen-Club website (sac-cas.ch).
- If you love the sport, check out the Helvetiq book *Via Ferrata* by Florian Müller & Sébastian Anex which profiles 30 via ferratas for all skill levels in Switzerland.

 ## Contact Details:

Imholz Sport Piazza Gottardo
Furkagasse 2
6490 Andermatt
+41 41 880 70 60
andermatt@imholzsport.ch
imholzsport-andermatt.ch

More K2 options:

+ Rotstock, Grindelwald, BE
+ Beginners and Fixed-Rope, Braunwald, GL
+ Via Ferrata Pinut, Flims, GR
+ Sulzfluh, St. Antönien, GR
+ Via Ferrata Belvédère, Nax, VS
+ Mini Fixed-Rope Trail, Saas-Grund, VS
+ Climbing/training area, Saas-Fee, VS (saas-fee.ch)
+ Rougemont, Château-d'Oex, VD

The Hike That has it All

CANTON: Valais
LOCATION: Fiesch

START AND END POINT: Belalp

6 HOURS

MEDIUM

▶ ▶ ▶ Best time of year:
JUNE–OCTOBER

AGE RANGE: 10+

EQUIPMENT: Hiking shoes, sun protection, water!

THE HIKE THAT HAS IT ALL

 Overview:

Some hikes are pure bliss and this is one of them. This vigorous, scenic, full-day hike is well worth the effort. It follows Aletsch Panoramaweg Route 39 and the area is a UNESCO World Heritage Site.

Turn right out of the Belalp lift station, uphill toward Hotel Belalp. Take the time to observe the picturesque chapel at Aletschbord perched on a nearby hill. As you drop down the mountain to officially begin the route, the inclination to take photos is ever-present.

In Belalp, you approach a vista that overlooks the valley with the stunning Aletsch Glacier. To the left is a White-Red-White trail to "Hängebrücke," one of the highlights of this hike. The Belalp-Riederalp suspension bridge is impressive: 124 m in length and 80 m above the Massa Gorge. Stop in the middle to grasp the magnificence of your current location. Cast your gaze up and down the valley and beneath you to the gorge below. The bridge is expansive and a genuine engineering feat.

Continue on a steady uphill climb that weaves through rocky paths, forests, and gorgeous terrain toward Rieder Furka and then Riederalp, where you find the Pro Natura Center, one of two national centers in Switzerland. Pro Natura has existed for over 100 years and strives to protect Switzerland's natural world. It's an organization worth supporting if you don't already.

The Pro Natura site in Valais is in a stately building known as Villa Cassel. This lovely spot is worth visiting and the modest museum in the building's basement provides a wealth of information. Entrance is free if you're a Pro Natura member. The center has been a nature reserve of Pro Natura's since 1933 and runs programs and tours in the area. If you're looking for a meal, coffee, or unique overnight accommodation, we recommend Villa Cassel.

THE HIKE THAT HAS IT ALL

After your visit, and once your hike is complete, make your way to your final destination via the Riederalp West or Riederalp Mitte lift stations. Hikes like this are beautiful gems, providing remarkable nature, adventurous opportunities, and the chance to gain a deeper appreciation of the environment.

Trail markers:

Belalp → Hotel Belalp → Hirmi → Licka → Nilti → Aletschji → Leng Acher → Teife Wald → Rieder Furka → Riederalp West

 ## Tips:

- Pick up local provisions for a picnic along the route. If you're lucky, the resident goats near the bridge might join you.
- Pack enough water and food for the entire day, layers of clothing and a first-aid kit.
- Never attempt this route in poor weather.
- Children doing this hike should be accustomed to long distances.

 ## Contact Details:

Pro Natura Center Aletsch
Villa Cassel
3987 Riederalp
+41 27 928 62 20
aletsch@pronatura.ch
pronatura-aletsch.ch

THE HIKE THAT HAS IT ALL

More options:

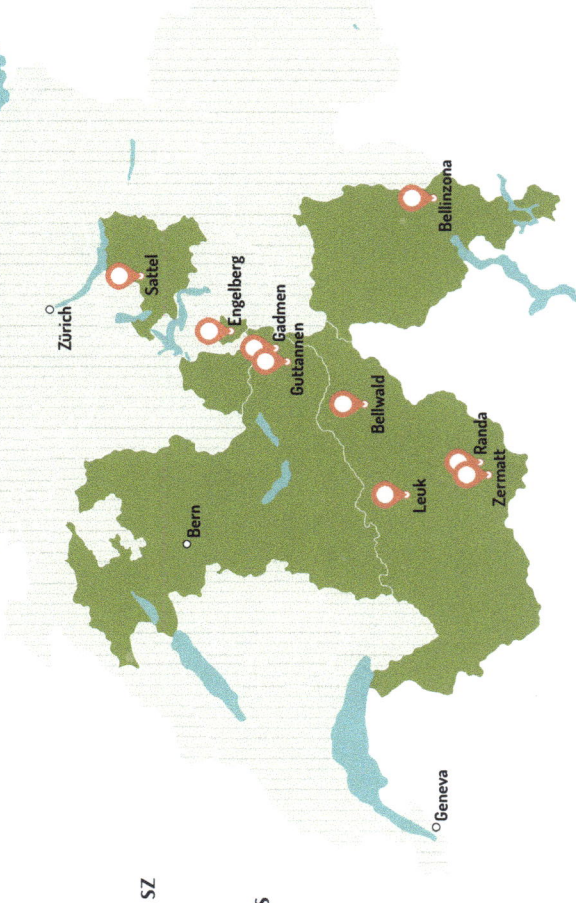

+ Trift Bridge, Gadmen, BE
+ Handeck Suspension Bridge, Guttannen, BE
+ Bhutan Bridge, Leuk, VS
+ Titlis Cliff Walk, Engelbgerg, OW
+ Raiffeisen Skywalk Suspension Bridge, Sattel, SZ
+ Ponte Tibetano Carasc, Bellinzona, TI
+ Goms Bridge, Bellwald, VS
+ Charles Kuonen Suspension Bridge, Randa, VS
+ Furi Hanging Bridge, Zermatt, VS

Aletsch Glacier Tour

CANTON: Valais
LOCATION: Fiesch

START AND END POINT: Fiesch Talstation

6 HOURS

HARD

▶ ▶ ▶ **Best time of year:**
JUNE–OCTOBER

AGE RANGE: 10+

EQUIPMENT: Hiking shoes, sun protection, water!

Overview:

The size and scale of the mighty Aletsch Glacier is a sight to behold. It's the longest in Europe at 20 km and is thousands of years old. While you can observe the glacier from three main viewing points (Bettmerhorn, Eggishorn and Moosfluh) there's something absolutely captivating about experiencing it on foot.

The Aletsch Glacier is part of the Jungfrau-Aletsch UNESCO World Heritage Site. Meet your tour guide and the rest of the group at the designated time in front of the Volken Sport store, inside Fiesch gondola station. After paying for the guided trip, purchase a gondola ticket and meet again up top at the Fiescheralp station. Everyone collects their equipment (crampons and harness) at the Gletscherstube Märjelen (this is also a great spot to have a coffee and cake after your trek) before heading down to the glacier.

Once on the ice, it's easy to feel as though the glacier has a life of its own. Magnificent blue colors and crevasses make for an exciting adventure. Your guide provides all the necessary safety information and interesting facts. The glacier moves approximately 100 m per year, or over 25 cm per day! Try to listen to the glacier moving: sometimes it sounds like a rockfall when it cracks and groans.

We are keenly aware that Switzerland's glaciers are under great pressure. We hope that by encouraging people to observe these mighty forces they'll be compelled to act. Global warming is drastically changing the Aletsch Glacier, as well as many glaciers in the Alps. The Pro Natura Center reports that the Aletsch Glacier is losing up to 50 m in length each year. Consider becoming a member of Pro Natura (pronatura.ch) or supporting the Glacier Initiative (gletscher-initiative. ch).

Tips:

+ There is often a cold breeze across the glacier. Dress appropriately.
+ Bring plenty of water, a packed lunch and snacks. You'll have lunch on the glacier.
+ Never go onto the glacier without a guide.
+ If you love this experience, you might want to do an extended version: a two-day guided crossing starting from Jungfraujoch, with an overnight stay in the historic Konkordia Hut, and ending in Fiescheralp (aletscharena.ch).
+ There's also a challenging four-day guided option from Jungfraujoch which crosses several glaciers to Grimsel Hospiz, BE (outdoor.ch).
+ While in the area, on a separate trip, visit Glacier World Bettmerhorn. Admission is free and there's a museum.

ALETSCH GLACIER TOUR

Contact Details:

Bergsteigerzentrum Aletsch
Fieschertalstrasse 1
3984 Fiesch
+41 27 971 17 76
info@bergsteigerzentrum.ch
bergsteigerzentrum.ch

More options:

+ **Gauli Glacier, BE** (gaulihuette.ch)
+ **Diavolezza Morteratsch Glacier hike, GR** (corvatsch-diavolezza.ch)
+ **Rhône Glacier, VS** (gletscher.ch; zermattersalpineschool.ch)
+ **Zinal Glacier, VS** (valdanniviers.ch)
+ **Gorner Glacier and Monta Rosa Hut, VS** (zermatters.ch)
+ **Ice Grotto of Mittelallalin, above Saas-Fee, VS** (saas-fee.ch)

Underground Lake

CANTON: Valais
LOCATION: St–Léonard

START AND END POINT:
Le Lac

45 MINUTES

EASY

▶ ▶ ▶ Best time of year:
MARCH–NOVEMBER

AGE RANGE:
4+

EQUIPMENT:
Warm jacket, sturdy shoes

Overview:

Just below the thriving vineyards in the lovely town of Saint-Léonard sits an underground lake that's been accessible to the public for more than 70 years. In 1946, when a major earthquake struck the area, the water level retreated, allowing access to the enchanting and magnificent lake below.

A series of stairs lead you down to the lake where you can take a 30-minute guided boat tour. As your guide explains this unique environment, you'll be enchanted by the crystal clear, 10°C water which is so pure you could drink it. Trout are now permanent lake residents and can be seen casually swimming just below the surface. Local white wine is still stored and aged, to this day, in the most unique setting: in barrels along the lake's end.

The geology of the area is impressive and the most common stones in the cave are marble, gypsum and shale. Water levels are higher in the spring due to snowmelt from the Alps and retreat as summer descends upon the valley. To date, this is one of the most expansive underground lakes in all of Europe. For the past several years, the water levels have been relatively low due to droughts in the region. Saint-Léonard is a true spectacle and certainly worthy of a visit.

 # Tips:

- From the bus stop, follow signs to Lac Souterrain. The bus stop is at the end of the road, Rue du Lac, just up the hill.
- The caves are open from 10:00–17:00 from mid- to late March until November. In July and August, opening hours are 9:00–17:30.
- Tickets must be purchased online prior to your visit. It's advised to arrive 15 minutes before your designated start time.
- There is a special SBB combination ticket for those traveling by train (sbb.ch).
- All tours are provided in three languages: German, French and English.
- The caves are chilly inside. Pack additional layers.
- A restaurant and toilets are onsite.

 # Contact Details:

Lac Souterrain de Saint-Léonard
Case postale 75, Rue du Lac 21
1958 Saint-Léonard
+41 27 203 22 66
admin@lac-souterrain.com
lac-souterrain.com

More options:

- While we would love to provide you with information about additional underground lakes in Switzerland, this is truly one of a kind. To learn more about caves, visit Höllgrotten Caves **(p. 183)** or St. Beatus Caves. (beatushoehlen.swiss).

Blacknose Sheep and Ziplines

CANTON:
Valais

LOCATION:
Zermatt

START AND END POINT:
Gornergrat

1 DAY

MEDIUM

▶ ▶ ▶ **Best time of year:**
JUNE–SEPTEMBER

AGE RANGE:
5+

EQUIPMENT:
Hiking shoes

Overview:

Zermatt has become famous for its adorable blacknose sheep. Learn more about these charming animals by taking the picturesque train from Zermatt to Gornergrat for the "Meet the Sheep" trail. There are 11 information stations (with QR codes for facts and videos) about these friendly animals.

The route is listed as moderate, with a total distance of just over 5.5 km. Plan roughly two hours or more to complete the downhill hike, which concludes at Riffelberg train station. The descent is about 600 m, so proper hiking shoes are a must.

For another fabulous experience, with the help of a GPS tracking system (don't forget your phone), guests might just get the chance to locate the sheep and the shepherdess from June to September. While the sheep are as friendly as dogs, please don't feed them.

Once you've seen the sheep, get ready for a thrilling adventure at the Forest Fun Park. Make your way from Zermatt train station toward the Zermatt gondola lift station. The park, just past and below the lift station, is not only a blast for those looking to push their climbing and zipline skills, but the views of the Matterhorn, Alpine peaks, and Matter Vispa River are breathtaking.

Tips:

- The Forest Fun Park is open daily from 10:00–19:00, including public holidays, from mid-May to October.
- Helmets, gloves and a climbing harness are provided.
- GPS signal to locate the sheep (sheep.gornergrat.ch; click the sheep icon located on the left on the map).
- There's a Kid's Trail for children aged 4+ and the Big Trail for children 8+.
- Training is provided before starting the rope courses. No previous experience is required.
- The maximum weight for the rope park is 120 kg.
- Groups of 10 or more need to reserve in advance.
- Lockers, toilets, food, and a picnic area are available at the train stations and the Forest Fun Park.

Contact Details:

Blacknose Sheep Theme Trail
(gornergrat.ch)

Forest Fun Park Zermatt
Steckenstrasse 110
3920 Zermatt
+41 27 968 1010
forestfunpark@gmail.com
zermatt-fun.com

BLACKNOSE SHEEP AND ZIPLINES

More options:

+ See our ibex and marmot tour in Pontresina, GR (p. 117)
+ Kronberg Zipline Park, Jakobsbad, AI
+ Adventure Park Adelboden, BE
+ Zipline Pradaschier, Churwalden, GR
+ Parc Aventure Chaumont, Neuchâtel, NE
+ Adventure Park Rheinfall, Neuhausen am Rheinfall, SH
+ Sternensauser Seilrutsche, Hoch-Ybrig, SZ
+ Flying Fox, Morschach, SZ
+ Adventure Park Gordola, TI
+ Monte Tamaro Zipline, Rivera, TI
+ Woufline de la Breya, Champex-Lac, VS
+ Grande Dixence AlpinLine, Lac des Dix, VS
+ Charmey Aventures, Val-de-Charmey, FR

Höllgrotten Caves

CANTON: Zug
LOCATION: Baar

START AND END POINT: Tobelbrücke–Höllgrotten

2–4 HOURS

EASY

▶ ▶ ▶ Best time of year:
APRIL–OCTOBER

AGE RANGE: 6+

EQUIPMENT: Waterproof jacket, sturdy shoes

Overview:

Caves offer a glimpse into a rare world and provide a peek into a subterranean universe. Switzerland is abundant with caves and Höllgrotten is a genuine site to behold. The dripstone formations were created thousands of years ago, and the venue opened to the public in 1887.

The caves were discovered when building the Bonstetten railway. Work was immediately stopped. The cave system is vast and now fully accessible to visitors thanks to a shaft connecting the two cave areas, which was built in 1917.

The Höllgrotten Caves offer visitors an outstanding journey through stalagmites and stalactites; all of which are surrounded by cloudy lakes. One of the most spectacular features here is the lighting. Vibrant colors of purple, blue, pink, green, make exploration a true delight. Grab the audio guide to learn more about the formation of the caves, including the fascinating geology of the area.

This area is rich with activities including biking (Lakes Route 7), hiking, barbecue facilities and swimming in the Lorze River. It's easy to plan the perfect day out!

The caves are a 25-minute walk from the bus stop. For the ultimate adventure, consider renting a scooter from Zugerberg and making the 1.5–2-hour journey to the caves (rother-events.ch/trotti-buchen). The caves are accessible by foot and bike from Baar. For bike rentals, consult the Zug Tourism bureau. Free parking is available at Lorzendamm 28, 6340 Baar, but be prepared to walk 3 km through the forest to reach the caves.

 ## Tips:

- **Check the website for opening hours, prices and discounts. Cash, Reka checks and most credit cards are accepted.**
- **Cave temperatures hover around 10°C.**
- **Guided tours are available.**
- **Toilets and a kiosk are located onsite.**

Contact Details:

Höllgrotten Baar Caves
6340 Baar
+41 41 761 83 70
info@hoellgrotten.ch
hoellgrotten.ch

More options:

+ Réclère Caves, Réclère, **JU** (prehisto.ch)
+ Underground mills, Col-des-Roches, **NE** (lesmoulins.ch)
+ Kobelwald crystal cave near Oberriet, **SG** (kristallhoehle.ch)
+ Hölloch, Muotatthal, **SZ** (trekking.ch/hoelloch)
+ Vallorbe Caves, Vallorbe, **VD** (grottesdevallorbe.ch)
+ Fairy's Cave, Saint-Maurice, **VS** (grotteauxfees.ch)

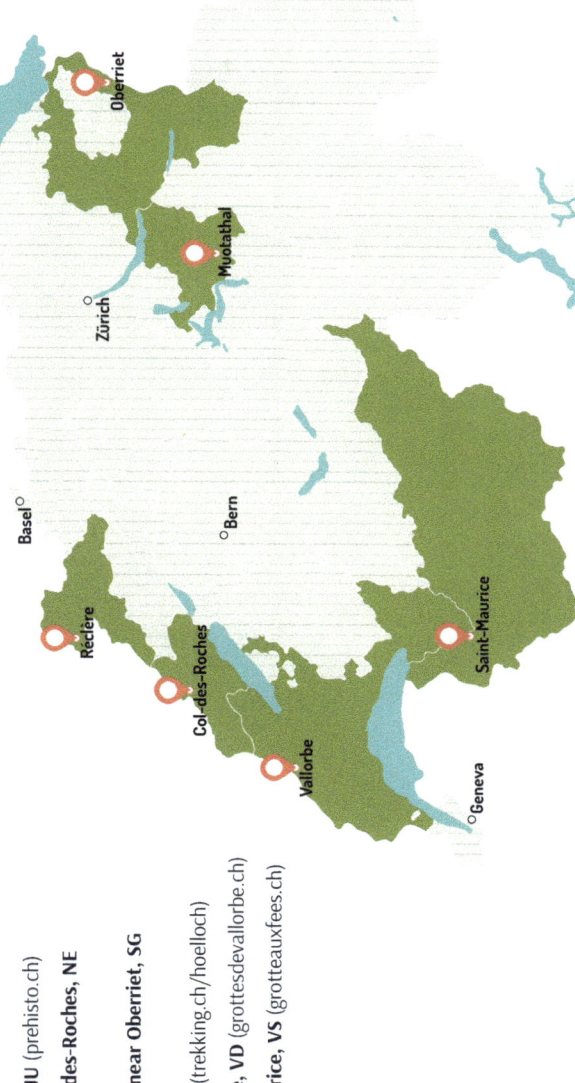

Disc Golf

1.5 HOURS

EASY

▶ ▶ ▶ Best time of year:
JUNE–OCTOBER

AGE RANGE:
5+

CHF

EQUIPMENT:
Hat, sunglasses, sturdy shoes

 **Contact:**
- discgolf.ch
- udisc.com
- mountaindiscs.ch

Overview:

Disc golf has the ability to transform a simple walk into a wild adventure. This sport dates back to 1976 and was created and patented in America by Ed Headrick. Originally, disc golf was loosely played by tossing frisbees into or at random targets.

Much like golf, the object of this game is relatively simple: get your disc (ball) into the metal basket (hole). When you hear the sound of your disc hitting the metal chains, you might just become addicted to the sport. We sure did!

There are typically nine or 18 baskets in a disc golf game. Your score card (collected at the time of rental) tells you the distance and "par," or number of throws required, for each hole. Don't worry if it takes you more tosses as there is a learning curve to the sport!

Please do not be fooled: the terrain is nothing like a traditionally groomed golf course. Each course is unique. They may be wooded, wild and/or hilly, with obstacles to navigate that make throwing your disc all the more exciting. The individual or team with the least number of throws wins. It's that simple.

There are more than 50 disc golf courses in Switzerland, making this inexpensive sport accessible to many.

 ## Tips:

- This sport is competitive, so get ready to level up!
- It can be played as single players or in groups: you decide!
- Allow 1.5 hours or more for a nine-hole course.
- A disc golf frisbee is quite different from a traditional frisbee.
- Inquire if you can rent your equipment at the location you plan to play.
- There are different types of discs that serve unique purposes. As novices, we opted for the two provided.
- Losing your disc is a possibility. Make sure you have a good spotter in the group!
- Pack water and snacks in case you're out there a long time.
- If you want to spend more time playing this sport (not hard to do), consider purchasing your own discs.
- Tournaments are held throughout the year.

Options:

- Disc Golf Pruntrutermatte, Basel, BS
- Disc Golf Parcours Gurten, Köniz, BE
- Disc Golf Parcours Alterswil, FR
- Disc Golf Parcours Sarasin, Grand-Saconnex, GE
- Disc Golf Parcours Filzbach, GL
- Disc Golf Davos, GR
- Disc Golf Parcours Stans, NW
- Disc Golf Parcours Neuenburg Parc de Pierre-à-Bot, Neuchâtel, NE
- Disc Golf Pizol, Bad Ragaz, SG
- Lila Disc Golf, Hofstetten-Flüh, SO
- Disc Golf Parcours Weinfelden, TG
- National Youth Sports Centre, Tenero-Contra, TI
- Disc Golf Loèche-les-Bains, Leukerbad, VS
- Disc Golf Pays-d'Enhaut, Chateau d'Oex, VD
- Disc Golf Mattenhof, Zurich, ZH

European Outdoor Film Tour

2–3 HOURS	**EASY**	

 ▶ ▶ ▶ Best time of year: **NOVEMBER–MARCH**

 **AGE RANGE: 10+**		 **EQUIPMENT:** Comfortable clothing

 Contact:

ch.eoft.eu

Overview:

The European Outdoor Film Tour (EOFT) is the perfect event for watching both extreme and everyday athletes from around the globe. The film tour has been in existence since 2001 and was launched by the Munich-based company Moving Adventures Media.

The EOFT takes place in major cities throughout Switzerland and Europe. Each year, it showcases "protagonists," or main characters, in an array of outdoor disciplines including skiing, kayaking, climbing, running, biking, paragliding, and more. Viewers receive an up close and personal look into the lives of the profiled athletes. By learning their personal stories, you gain a better understanding of what motivates them to achieve their most tenacious goals. This film festival leaves you pining to spend more time outdoors.

Multiple films are shown throughout the evening. The cinematography we saw was spectacular and the athletes' stories uplifting: the night was a genuine treat. The athletes defy the impossible and push personal limits to achieve their wildest ambitions; if that's not inspirational, we don't know what is!

If you're looking to up your adventure game, or simply want to learn from some of the most inspiring athletes on the planet, do yourself a favor and attend this awesome film tour. While we're sad we only discovered EOFT in 2022, we're definitely returning!

 ## Tips:

- Arrive early to select the best seats. There are no assigned seats at the venues.
- Ticket prices vary for adults, children and groups.
- The event is several hours in duration with a short intermission. Food and drinks are available.
- If you bring a backpack, it must be checked in.
- The films might have colorful language. This is to be expected as the athletes participate in some pretty gnarly adventures!
- Commentary at each event is a lovely addition.
- A special app can be downloaded to assist with audio subtitles. This information is provided by EOFT.
- The event soundtrack is available on the EOFT website. It's a pretty awesome selection of music!

Geocaching

COURSE-DEPENDENT

EASY

▶ ▶ ▶ **Best time of year:**

ALL YEAR

AGE RANGE:

5+

EQUIPMENT:

Sturdy shoes, phone, app, power bank

 **Contact:**

 geocaching.com

 @GoGeocaching

 @geocaching

App Geocaching, Cachly, Adventure Lab

Overview:

What is geocaching? If you've never heard of it, you're in for a surprise. We classify geocaching as an outdoor adventure that leads participants to treasures, known as geocaches or caches. Geocaches come in different shapes and sizes and once you're aware that they exist, you might just spot them everywhere. Geocaching is a global treasure hunt which currently takes place in over 190 countries and kicked-off in the early 2000s. Geocaching has attracted quite the following since.

Using a smart phone and an app, you're given clues which lead you to official geocaching logbooks, tiny boxes, or geocache treasures. You're able to determine the level of difficulty pertaining to the hidden cache, the size of the cache you're searching for, and the terrain or area in which the cache has been hidden.

Geocaching is ideal for those looking to spend time outdoors, but long for more than a mere stroll in the woods. This exciting adventure leads you through forests, over hills, beside lakes, and into cities on the search for the next treasure. It's an ideal way to learn or teach people how to navigate and become more familiar with the area where they live!

Geocaching makes for a fabulous group activity by encouraging you to explore a new city, or simply slow down on a relaxing Sunday. Get excited about your next outdoor experience with geocaching!

 # Tips:

- To play, you must first create a free account at geocaching.com or by using one of the free apps.
- The paid app version has more cache locations and extra features.
- Play individually, while on a date (cool idea), or in teams.
- Once you successfully navigate to your first geocache, sign the logbook and mark your discovery online.
- In some cases, you might just discover a tiny prize hidden inside. If there is a prize, it's then your duty to replace it: take a prize, leave a prize is the general rule.
- Always return the geocache exactly how it was discovered out of courtesy for the next person.
- Not all locations are easy to access, requiring participants to wander off the main path. Respect the environment when you do, as some locations are in nature habitats.
- When searching in urban environments, be discreet! Wait until there is no one around to find the hidden cache. This ensures that strangers or non-players do not remove the cache!

Sleeping Under the Stars

 **START AND END POINT:** *Any Place Above 2000 m*	 **1 NIGHT**	 **MEDIUM**

 ▶ ▶ ▶ **Best time of year:** **JUNE–SEPTEMBER**

 **AGE RANGE:** **5+**		 **EQUIPMENT:** Hiking shoes, sleeping bag, tent, water, food, first-aid kit

SLEEPING UNDER THE STARS

Overview:

There is a genuine allure to wild camping. Sleeping under the stars provides a sense of total freedom, which washes over you as night blankets the Alps. For some, this is a primal calling. Before you consider this adventure, please know how Switzerland perceives it: wild camping or bivouacking are not essentially illegal, but not a highly favored activity either. Exceptions are made when treks take longer than anticipated or inclement weather kicks in. If you plan to camp, please do so with ultimate respect.

If you're looking for this book to call out and identify the ideal places to sleep in the wild, we cannot do that. That would cause a large human footprint in particular areas. We understand that wild camping is a controversial issue in Switzerland and do not recommend that individuals wild camp on a regular basis; however, we make every attempt to list the necessary rules for those who wish to partake in this activity out of necessity or pleasure. Please use this as a guide for how to properly engage in an overnight outdoors.

The best tip we can give on wild camping is to do so only when absolutely necessary. Switzerland has a robust hut system, so opt for staying in one of the many (153 Swiss Alpine Club) huts or spectacular mountain inns. Detailed information about hut locations is in *Fresh Air Kids Switzerland – Hikes to Huts*.

Tips:

+ You should only camp above the tree line, which is roughly 2000 m.
+ Never attempt to camp in a protected wildlife zone.
+ Camping is not permitted in national parks and nature reserves.
+ Cantons have their own rules and regulations about sleeping outdoors. Know them before you go! Inquire with local tourist offices or municipal offices to determine if it's permissible to camp in your intended location.
+ If you plan to sleep near a hut or mountain inn, ask permission before doing so.
+ Do not start any campfires. Respect all posted signs in the area, especially when it comes to fire bans.
+ Bury your toilet waste and never urinate or use soap close to a natural water source.
+ Remove all trash and indications of your stay.
+ Pay attention to any native plants and animals in the area and do no harm to either.
+ If you plan to camp for more than one night, pack away your tent every morning.
+ Not disclosing your location on social media helps protect and preserve natural and wild spaces.

SLEEPING UNDER THE STARS

Options:

- **A comprehensive list of camping locations in Switzerland** (camping.info)
- **Camp sites in Switzerland, Germany and Austria** (gocamping.ch)
- **TCS camp sites** (tcs.ch)
- **Aaregg Familencampingplatz, Brienz, BE** (aaregg.ch)
- **Camping Seegärtli, Brienz, BE** (camping-seegaertli.ch)
- **Nature camping spots, GR** (graubuenden.ch)
- **Ticino camping, TI** (ticino.ch)
- **Yurt camping, Sufers, SZ** (zelter.ch)

Tour de Suisse

2-3 HOURS

EASY

▶ ▶ ▶ **Best time of year: JUNE**

AGE RANGE: All

EQUIPMENT: Sun/rain protection

Contact:

tourdesuisse.ch

Overview:

The Tour de Suisse started in 1933, and while not as old as the Tour de France and Giro d'Italia, our road cycling race also includes time trials and grueling mountain stages. Competitors come from over two dozen nations and in 2022, for the first time in Tour de Suisse history, welcomed women; making the race an inclusive event.

If you have yet to take in the athleticism and excitement of a Tour de Suisse, mark your calendars for June! While all stages are a genuine inspiration to witness, in our humble opinion, watching riders complete a stage is absolute frenzied excitement! The noise from the cheering crowds and the "hopp, hopp" is contagious. Bring a cowbell or horn to cheer them on as they sprint to the finish line.

The route for the Tour de Suisse changes each year. Check the website to preview the race schedule, which is published approximately one month before the tour starts. The best viewing locations vary, depending on the type of stage. If the day includes a time trial (individual or team) you can watch at various locations as riders are always on route. If the day includes a criterium (many loops in the same location) try to position yourself near the finish line. For stage race days (point to point), crowds gather around the finish line. If you venture a bit past the finish line, near the team zone (where the buses are parked), you might see the riders up close.

 # Tips:

- If you have biking enthusiasts in your house, this is the event for you! If not, it's still incredibly cool to witness.
- Use public transport. Parking anywhere can be challenging due to the number of support vehicles and road closures.
- Never cross the path of the riders to get to the other side of the road.
- Small children might benefit from noise canceling headphones, as the event is very loud!
- Pack water and snacks.
- Toilets aren't always easily accessible.
- The event runs in all types of weather conditions.

Other options:

- **Giro d'Italia in May** (giroditalia.it)
- **Tour de France in July** (letour.fr)
- **Tour de France Femmes end of July** (letourfemmes.fr)

CHAPTER IV

THE TRANSFORMATIVE POWER OF THE MINI ADVENTURE

> "
> Adventure is just about doing something you've never done—doing it with enthusiasm and curiosity; doing something difficult with passion.
> "
>
> ALASTAIR HUMPHREYS
> AUTHOR, ADVENTURER,
> MOTIVATIONAL SPEAKER

Not every day affords us the luxury of participating in a grand adventure. That's where the mini adventure comes in. Mini adventures serve the purpose of encouraging us to experience new opportunities close to home and without having to spend a fortune. They break up our normal routines by inspiring connection to our local landscapes. By doing so, life becomes pretty exciting!

The best time to participate in any kind of adventure is now! In winter, spring, summer or fall, outdoor activities are waiting. If you need to squeeze in an adventure, consider the early morning hours before your daily tasks begin. Nothing makes you feel more alive than starting your day with an exciting opportunity that propels you out of bed. If time is tight in the morning, consider an activity after work and/or on the weekends. Don't just save adventures for holidays, because a memorable experience can take place anytime, especially in Switzerland!

Here's our list of adventures that can be completed anytime, anywhere as most of them are free!

- Strap on your headlamp and head outside for a night hike in a familiar area.
- Witness the sunrise from a local mountain, vista or bridge.
- Build a campfire (where it's legal) and barbecue. Invite friends and make an afternoon of it!
- Go outside and enjoy warm summer rain.
- Swim in cold water to feel remarkably alive.
- Geocache in your neighborhood and be amazed at what you discover.
- Visit a local botanical garden. Try to learn the names of three new flowers.
- Visit a local farm and talk to the farmer.
- Make it your mission to identify native plant species in your area.
- Participate in a full moon walk.
- Search for or listen for nocturnal animals in a local forest.
- Kayak or canoe.
- Swim in a local river or body of water.
- Forest bathe. You don't need an expert to guide you through the forest, simply find an area you're familiar with and notice your breath, the trees around you, and pay close attention to how you feel, your heartrate and your level of relaxation. For more, consider reading *Walking in the Woods* by Professor Yoshifumi Miyazaki.
- Sleep outside.
- Grab your camera and head outdoors. Whether in an urban or natural setting, pick a theme (bugs, plants, birds, flowers, buildings, architecture, colors, shapes, etc.) and try to capture the area through a whole new lens.

- Visit an area in your hometown you have yet to see.
- Scoot, bike or walk to work. Take a new route instead of the routine.
- Sleep in an exciting new location. Think garden, balcony, campground, tiny house, beach, tree house, etc.
- Do something you would normally never do in a season that feels ridiculous to do it!
- Visit a new museum or a special exhibition.
- Make a list of "I have never…" for example, swum in my local river, camped in a tent, made dinner outside, night hiked. Challenge yourself to complete them all.
- Enjoy an outdoor picnic by candlelight.
- Celebrate a birthday outdoors!
- Find a local creek and walk barefoot.
- Get your bike ready and head out for a 50 km bike challenge.
- Drive on a local pass. Our top recommendation is the Grimsel Pass. Visit the Rhône Glacier while there.
- Play! As adults, we often neglect play. Don't let this happen to you and remember to be as inquisitive as a child.
- Visit a local trash processing plant or recycling center.
- Plant a garden regardless of where you live.
- Grab your telescope and witness the stars like never before. If you need some inspiration, check out the Basel Astronomy Association (astronomie-basel.ch).
- Jump on a train with no particular destination in mind.
- Strap on your hiking boots and head out for the day. Bring a well-stocked backpack, a map or a cell phone and make it your mission to spend the day exploring.
- Locate nature reserves close to home. Explore those new areas with friends or family.
- Participate in a local clean-up day. Consider Trash Heroes (trashhero.org/category/trash-hero-switzerland) or the Summit Foundation (summit-foundation.org) which organize clean ups.
- Swim in a local pool.
- Visit a local farmer's market and buy a fruit or vegetable you have never tried.
- Witness a festival in your area.
- Go to an outdoor movie. Basel hosts a spectacular event each year in August.

CHAPTER V

THE BEST OF OUR ADVENTURES

> "
> The sun will rise and set regardless. What we choose to do with the light while it's here is up to us. Journey wisely.
> "
>
> **ALEXANDRA ELLE**
> AUTHOR, EDUCATOR, PODCAST HOST

 # The Best Of Our Adventures:

Our Favorite Water Activity

Noah: Stand-up paddleboarding
Tessa: Whitewater rafting
Robert: Glacier crossing
Melinda: Rhine River swim

Our Favorite Land Activity

Noah: Riding different tracks at the Swiss Bike Park
Tessa: Trotti bikes
Robert: All of our underground visits
Melinda: The hike and overnight to Faulhorn.

Our Favorite Air Activity

Noah: Ziplines at Forest Fun Park in Zermatt
Tessa: Balmberg rope park was awesome!
Robert: Paragliding
Melinda: Paragliding. Speechless!

The Activity that Made us Long for More

Noah: Stand-up paddleboarding is pretty awesome!
Tessa: I would like to do more whitewater rafting
Robert: The First to Faulhorn hiking tour
Melinda: I'd have to say the thrill of paragliding!

The Adventure that Evoked the Greatest Sense of Awe

Noah: Seeing wild ibex
Tessa: Watching my parents paraglide
Robert: The Alpine mountain bike tour
Melinda: Watching the sunrise at Faulhorn. Sweet, sweet memories

Best Adventure Advice

Noah: Discover new things!
Tessa: It's important to try new things
Robert: Embrace the unknown. Life is an adventure; just go for it!
Melinda: In the end, we regret only that which we did not do

Most Humbling Moment

Noah: I kept losing my ball during Swin Golf
Tessa: The experience at the Blindekuh
Robert: Weather changes overhead while on a via ferrata
Melinda: Not much more to say than ... via ferrata!

Hilarious Moment

Noah: Lake Murten Bike Tour. We are the fast chaps!
Tessa: Whitewater rafting with our friends
Robert: Making new friends on the highway in our Cheeky campervan
Melinda: Disc Golf was a fantastic experience!

Our Next Big Adventure

Noah: I want to paraglide
Tessa: Horseback riding at night!
Robert: Completing everything on our "To Do" list
Melinda: The possibilities are endless!

THE BEST OF OUR ADVENTURES

Epilogue:

We're still smiling after all the adventures that unfolded during the creation of this book. We've learned, explored, tested our limits, and been humbled on more than one occasion. Sometimes, we walked away from excursions feeling absolutely spent and rendered speechless; upon reflection, those were some of our very best days. As always, Mother Nature reminded us that, despite our meticulous planning, she is the one in charge.

We leave this experience with a fresh appreciation for the natural world and the very spaces that call to us, whispering our names, begging us to return. While we continue to eagerly answer the call, perhaps it's now time to take a breath to contemplate what's next. Regardless of where the road may lead, our lives are all the richer for each and every experience. We know so much more awaits.

Melinda and Robert Schoutens have spent nearly two decades connecting deeply with the natural world. The Swiss mountains have become their favorite place to spend time as a family. As their children have aged, Alpine adventures are what they seek. Whether that be spending the night in a remote Alpine hut, visiting a rope park, swimming in an Alpine lake, or simply enjoying a mountain meal, they are always their happiest when they are exploring the Swiss Alps.

With Helvetiq, they have published: *Fresh Air Kids Switzerland, Fresh Air Kids Switzerland – Hikes to Huts*, and *Winter Kids Switzerland* with the mission to inspire families and individuals to connect with nature one outdoor experience at a time.

Fresh Air Kids Switzerland
52 Inspiring Hikes That Will
Make Kids and Parents Happy
ISBN: 978-2-940481-62-0

Fresh Air Kids Switzerland
Hikes to Huts
ISBN: 978-3-907293-23-2

Winter Kids Switzerland
36 Family Activities
ISBN: 978-3-907293-88-1

To follow the latest adventures of the authors visit:

 @fresh_air_kids

For recommended locations, experiences, adventures, and more visit:

 freshairkids.com

www.ingramcontent.com/pod-product-compliance
Lightning Source LLC
Chambersburg PA
CBHW061254230426
43665CB00027B/2947